Randall Pitts

LIFE UNDER COMPULSION

Ten Ways to Destroy the Humanity of Your Child

ANTHONY ESOLEN

ISI
BOOKS

Wilmington, Delaware

Library of Congress Cataloging-in-Publication Data

Esolen, Anthony M.
  Life under compulsion : ten ways to destroy the humanity of your child / Anthony Esolen. —
1 Edition.
     pages cm
  Includes index.
  ISBN 978-1-61017-094-9 (hardback)
  1. Child rearing. 2. Parenting. 3. Education. 4. Child development. I. Title.
  HQ769.E767 2015
  649'.1 — dc23
                              2015006264

Published in the United States by:

ISI Books
Intercollegiate Studies Institute
3901 Centerville Road
Wilmington, Delaware 19807-1938
www.isibooks.org

Manufactured in the United States of America

For my wife, Debra,
the maker and the keeper of our home

Contents

LIFE UNDER COMPULSION

Introduction

Life Under Compulsion

The trouble with language is that you can use it not only to reveal the truth but also to conceal it or distort it. We are taken in by words. In the Garden of Eden the serpent said to Eve, "Ye shall be as gods," and Eve was too eager to pause to examine the meaning of the word *gods*, or why Satan used the plural rather than the singular. Most of the harm that we suffer by misused language comes not from conscious liars, like the serpent, but from ourselves, from an unconscious and persistent tendency to reverse the order of reality and language. Words take the place of things. We hear the word *education* and think immediately of our state-ordered system of schools, where little that merits the name of education may be going on. We hear the word *equality* and immediately think of the justice of the civil rights movement, and we do not pause to ask what is equal to what, or even whether the things we are equating are commensurable.

I believe that the same automatism has taken over the word *freedom*, which now means for most of us a mere permission slip guaranteed by the state. I am writing this book because I believe we are bringing our children up not for the freedom we enjoy but for the compulsions we suffer. Some of those compulsions we even mistake for freedom, so that the more of them we win, the more tightly we bind ourselves, body and soul.

What do I mean by the word *compulsion*? Let's consider a few situations in which the auxiliary verb *must* comes into play:

• Pa has been surprised by a blizzard on his way walking from town to his homestead on the prairie. He cannot see more than a foot in front of him. He has no way of telling whether he is walking toward home or away from it or in circles. Eventually he falls through a snow crust into a hollow where the air is good. The snow is heaped up around and above him, a good eight or nine feet high. He knows that he *must* stay there to wait out the blizzard, though that may take days. He tries very hard not to eat the oyster crackers that he was bringing back as a Christmas treat, but after a day or two he can no longer hold out. His body commands him. He *must* have something to eat.

• An uncle is writing to his nephew, giving him advice on how to lead his "patient" to damnation. He recommends bringing the patient into company with "friends" who are worldly and flippant, whose conversation is predictable in its sophistry, who are conformists of nonconformity, and who never think of God without the automatic irony of feeling superior to the lowly people who believe in Him. The nephew should lead the patient into the *habits* of these friends, "and as habit," he says, "renders the pleasures of vanity and excitement and flippancy at once less pleasant and harder to forgo . . . you will find that anything or nothing is sufficient to attract his wandering attention. . . . You can make him waste his time not only in conversation he enjoys with people whom he likes, but in conversations with those he cares nothing about on subjects that bore him." The patient will do these things because he *must*, though he may never actually hear a command telling him so.

• A man has made his name feared by all the people in the country around him. He dwells on a mountain in an impregnable fortress, manned by his ruffians and villains. He sometimes does things that redound to justice, from the sheer pleasure of exercising his power; more often, though, he exercises his power "on behalf of evil intentions, atrocious revenges, or tyrannical caprice." He has taken delight "to do whatever the laws forbade," and now, after many years, it has become automatic in him. He has promised a subordinate baron to kidnap a pious girl from a convent, where she is in hiding. The baron wants to ravish her. The warlord's ruffians do kidnap the girl, but they are moved by her weeping and her promise to pray for them. The warlord begins to feel uneasy. "I *must* be rid of her," he says to himself, when all at once "another voice from within him replied with a resounding 'No!'" He *must not* give the girl to the baron.

• The pilgrim Dante is with his guide Beatrice in Paradise. They are standing before the souls of the wise, who appear to them as stars of surpassing light. Someone must reveal to Dante who they are. One of the twelve souls thus comes forward and, knowing how ardently Dante longs to know their names, and how bountifully the grace of God has been poured upon him, says this:

> He who'd deny his flask of wine to slake
> your thirst would not be free, would have such power
> as rivers not returning to the sea.

He simply *must* answer love with love. If he did not comply with that *must*, he would not be acting as a free soul. The saint who speaks is Thomas Aquinas.

Let us look at the four cases. The first, from Laura Ingalls Wilder's autobiographical *Little House on the Prairie*, describes a hardy and virtuous man in a dangerous situation. He is motivated at all moments by a perfectly reasonable and just desire to preserve himself from death, and by his love for his family. His body cries out for food. What he does in eating the oyster crackers is trivial enough, and because it was so trivial, he could not hold out. Had it been instead the difference between life and death for his family, he would never have eaten the crackers. His body overrules him—but his reason allows it. It is also an unusual circumstance. We do not often find ourselves in snow caves in the midst of a blizzard. This is not what I am calling compulsion.

The fourth case, that of Dante before the blessed souls, might look like compulsion to the modern reader, and that is why I include it here. Thomas Aquinas expresses the paradox quite well. To be "free" is not to do as you please but rather to realize the fulfillment of your natural and created being, without impediments. To admit those impediments would be to compromise your freedom. It would be like cutting your own hamstrings. So when love is offered, the free heart, unimpeded by niggling selfishness, responds in love. When truth is asked for, the free mind, seeing truth clearly and not wishing to duck under a covert, speaks the truth. To will to do otherwise would be like willing that you were not the kind of being you are. You would then be a self-contradiction. The river flows naturally to the sea; its nature impels it to do so. Man's nature impels him to love what is beautiful and to seek the truth. That drive for love and truth is itself his liberty. This drive is natural and good. The river should not be blocked up with mud. Thomas Aquinas *must greet love with love, because he is free.* This is not what I am calling compulsion.

The second and third cases are very different. Let us go to the second. The habitually worldly do not feel themselves to be compelled at all. They are heedless in their flippancy. They seem to have before them a smorgasbord of choices. Shall they fornicate today? Shall they make fun of Christians? Shall they blow a nice sum of money on a trifle? Shall they spread ugly truths about someone of their acquaintance? Shall they jest about people of lesser intelligence, who believe in such things as honor and duty and love of country? Shall they teach their students how to enjoy semipornographic books? Shall they cast a film of cynicism over their young souls?

The sheer range of choices available to them convinces them that they are free. But they dwell in a cramped world, spiritually and intellectually and humanly speaking. They are in the deadly habit of simultaneously exalting themselves and making themselves puny. Whenever the beautiful or the mysterious threatens, they must duck back into the tortoise shell of the small-minded. They are quite predictable. They may have the money to travel all the world over, but they inevitably bring themselves along when they do, so they might have done better to stay home. Having clogged up their ears against the whispering of the divine, they are easy prey to the transient—exactly as Uncle Screwtape points out to his demon nephew in advising how to deal with his "patient." Their incapacity is both symptom and disease. They live the Life Under Compulsion.

The third case, from Alessandro Manzoni's historical novel *The Betrothed*, is a case study in compulsion. The warlord, the Unnamed, has used his considerable strength of will to bind himself to evil deeds. He has power in that he can call on brigands to enforce his will. But he has no power. For years he has almost mechanically gone on with his habits and has had to confirm one evil deed with another, one outrageous exercise of power with another, lest those around him cease to fear him. Now when he is faced with a simple girl, utterly innocent, whose prayer for the evil can elicit no vindictive and automatic response in him, he feels that he *must* be rid of her, lest his whole life begin to crumble about him. But a divine voice breaks into the self-made prison of his evil thoughts, commanding, *No! You must not!* If he obeys that command, if he allows himself to be ruled, he will begin the long process of breaking his Life Under Compulsion.

The compulsions I am talking about in this book not only make us less than heroes; they also make us less than human. They bind us to automatisms. They give us choice in what is evil or foolish or trivial, just as the keepers of an asylum will let their charges watch television or play poker for pennies. In fact, the keepers want them to do those things so they will be more comfortable in their imprisonment. *Dummheit macht frei*—stupidity or stolidity sets you "free."

Raising the Walls of the Asylum

"Get ready for a better world."

The motto belongs not to political revolutionaries or Silicon Valley visionaries but to a children's theme park popular in more than a dozen countries, and coming soon to a city near you. This park is not like the other entertainment options available to families. Children here do not scamper onto roller coasters; they pretend to be adults. As a reporter from the *New Yorker* described it, "children can work on a car assembly line, or move furniture, or put out a fake fire with real water." Through role playing in adult occupations, they earn a "salary" that can be "deposited in the central bank and accessed with a realistic-looking debit card"—after a "tax" of 20 percent is deducted. ("Here is a fun way we teach them to pay tax," says the company's founder and CEO.) Their pretend money can be used to purchase goods and services at stores operated by very real corporate sponsors—Sony, McDonald's, Coca-Cola, Domino's Pizza, and many others. (The park offers "a good platform in terms of building brand loyalty," another executive boasts.)

This theme park, unusual though it may be in its field, reflects an understanding of childhood that has become all too common. It is childhood as mere preparation for adulthood, and a dull, drab limited adulthood at that. Every year millions of parents take their children to this theme park, happily handing over the large admission fee, so that their children can...what? So they can take their position on an assembly line, or deliver packages, or prepare fast food, or make plastics, to earn enough to amass the latest consumer gadgets and pay their taxes to an unseen government overlord. Here we see a firm commitment to the tyranny of the *useful*. Consider: Children attending the theme park quickly learn that the less interesting the job, the more it pays. And the adult staffers end their conversations with children by saying, "Have a *productive* day."

How is this theme park creating a "better world"? The CEO has the answer: "We are empowering [children] to become independent."

Independence. Freedom. Liberty. These have become bywords of our time. And yet we hardly understand the terms at all anymore. Children are often called *our greatest resource*, as if they were deposits of tin. But a child is not (just as an adult is not) a lever in an economic machine, a vehicle for commerce, a revenue source for the all-powerful state. He is a human being, made in the image and likeness of God—made, that is, for goodness and truth and beauty.

But those concepts have disappeared in the contemporary celebration of "freedom." The assumption is now nearly automatic that freedom is without substance. It is an extrinsic condition, and a negative at that. It means that there are no strings upon the autonomous self. It is, as I have suggested above, freedom as license, as a permission slip to do as you please. It is freedom that worships the abstraction of choice: choice is the only thing that matters; whether it is one choice or another matters not at all.

This narrow and misguided understanding of freedom is now pervasive, but it is not new. Milton's Satan, having fallen from Heaven to Hell, looks about to find a dismal place, flat and dreary, a land of sulfurous bogs and bitumen, marl instead of good soil, stench instead of fresh air. But he remains undaunted, or strives hard to appear so. "Here at least," he says, "*we shall be free.*"

This is the assertion of an incorrigible brat. No one, not God Himself, can tell Satan what to do. That is why Satan calls the angel Gabriel a "proud limitary Cherub," sneering at his exercise of authority within the limits prescribed by God. It's also why the fellow demon Mammon advises against repentance, which, even if it were possible, would force "new subjection" on them, in which they would sing to God "forced Hallelujahs" and send up to Him their "servile offerings." In Hell, says Mammon, they will be "free and to none accountable," preferring "Hard liberty before the easy yoke / Of servile pomp."

But how much "liberty" does such substanceless freedom offer? "Nobody can tell me what to do," says the adolescent, except that everyone is ceaselessly at his ear, urging him, enticing him, rasping him, needling him, goading him, telling him that unless he *does something*, anything, he will waste his life, he will be *no one*. And the *something* that he absolutely must do is invariably political, narrowly defined, or economic, narrowly defined, or sexual, mechanically defined. He must rule, or make money, or "perform."

Welcome to Life Under Compulsion.

The compulsions that are enslaving so many of our children are of two kinds. Some compulsions come *from without*: government mandates that determine what children are taught, how they are taught, and even what they can eat in school. (The Latin root that gives us *compulsion* also gives us the *compulsory* in "compulsory education.") The only way you can get people en masse to submit to madness is by compulsion, because if you let them carry on their own affairs, in their own small locales and in their homes and in the sanctuary of their hearts, they will revert to nature, fallen as it may be. A system as insane as communism could survive only by making people believe that two and two are five, and by sending them to freeze in Siberia if they insisted that it was not so. Today we celebrate the "freedom" that we enjoy, turning for assurance to the electoral apparatus, a mechanical device on which we depend for what it cannot deliver. Men in a healthier time spent hardly a day in the year fretting about who sat in the office on Pennsylvania Avenue. And there was no need to fret, since the president's government encroached very little on human life. Now we devote endless time and attention to the subject—commercials, polls, news about polls, polls about news, polls about polls, news about news. And now that governmental machine controlled by the president dictates—compels—so much of how we live our lives.

There is a second kind of compulsion, the kind that comes *from within*: the itches that must be scratched, the passions by which children (like the rest of us) can be mastered. Spiritual compulsion is not the same thing as habit. It is not so much what the soul possesses as what possesses the soul. Compulsion is to a natural habit as lust is to love. The wretched souls in Dante's *Inferno*, when the boatman Charon tells them where they are going, curse God and their parents and the whole human race and the place and time of their begetting and their birth. They hate the hell they are about to enter. But they desire that same hell; they approach the boats like birds responding to the call of the fowler. "What they fear turns into their desire," says Virgil. So we see when we meet them down below. Ugolino *must* gnaw the brains of the archbishop Ruggieri, and with every clench of the teeth he must recall how his own treachery helped to cause the deaths of his innocent sons. Satan *must* flap his wings, eternally, trying to rise in defiance of God, yet raising the gale that freezes him in place.

So it is in our world today. We *must* respond immediately to the buzzing that signals a new text message, a new e-mail, a new social media post. We *must* click on the link, which promises quick gratification. We *must* buy the latest this or that vanity. We *must* be bound to the instant urge, wherever it may be found. Our mass entertainment, mass education, and mass politics cater to these compulsions, as the executives and corporate sponsors of our children's theme park understand all too well.

The Questions That Matter

How to raise children who can sit with a good book and read? Who are moved by beauty? Who delight in innocence? Who can walk outdoors and enjoy the beauty of weeds and sparrows? Who still possess youth, which lends them both a frolic childlikeness and a wisdom beyond their years? Who have no compulsions—who *don't* have to attend to the constant buzzing of a smartphone, or click on the next link and the next link and the next link, or buy the latest gadget, or submit to the instant urge?

These questions pass unnoticed by technocratic utilitarians left and right, by the "progressives" who have to move, move, move, who knows where, and even by lovers of the humanities, who don't wish to acknowledge the disease, because we all are infected.

But they are the questions that matter. Even more to the point: What sort of child shall you raise, my readers?

To resist Life Under Compulsion, to raise children who can throw off the shackles and enjoy truly free, and full, lives, we must affirm the old meaning of the English word *free*, which is related to joy and greatness of heart—associations now dim in English but still clear to our German cousins: *freude*, joy; *frieden*, peace. "Freely ye have received," says Jesus to His disciples; "freely give." He does not mean that the apostles should charge no fees for their teaching. He means to invite them into relationships of love. They have received the love of God freely; it is not compelled. He wants them to be *free* with themselves, to have free hearts for the love of others, bringing a peace that is full and alive, not merely the absence of war.

This older, fuller meaning points to the practical contradiction at the heart of the vision of freedom as noninterference. Unless we are to live as beasts ranging the fields, we must have order. But order implies hierarchy, those who must govern and those who must be governed. These groups may overlap considerably in one respect or another: even a senator is not supposed to cheat on his taxes, and even a day laborer can (still) tell his small son when it is time to go to bed. Obedience is inevitable. Satan himself says, when it suits his purposes, that "Orders and Degrees / Jar not with liberty, but well consist."

Freedom, in the end, is an intrinsic virtue, not an extrinsic condition, an accident of politics. It is not a negative—freedom *from*. Instead it is a positive—freedom *for*. This freedom is not for oneself but for others. Our bonds and responsibilities do not constrict our freedom but rather define our very humanity.

When the pilgrim Dante stands upon the shores of the Mountain of Purgatory, he looks to the heavens and sees the beautiful morning star in the East:

> The radiant planet fostering love like rain,
> made all the orient heavens laugh with light,
> veiling the starry Fishes in her train.

It is Venus, the star of love. What should that have to do with Purgatory? Everything, as it turns out, for evil clamps the heart and crushes the soul. To free oneself *from* the accumulated sludge of sin is to free oneself *for* the freedom of heart that is love. "He seeks his freedom," says Virgil to Cato, the guardian of Purgatory, as he begs to allow Dante to climb the mountain. Virgil does not mean that Dante is looking for a democratic republic. He wishes for Dante to learn about sin, but more, to learn about the wonders of love. He wishes for Dante to grow wings, so to speak. Without wings, you may say that you are free to fly, and say it all day long, but you will not get one foot off the ground.

On this matter the great pagans and the Christians, the poets and the philosophers, speak with one voice. In his soaring dialogue of love, the *Phaedrus*, Plato says that the soul in love grows wings, and that this is actually the purpose of a truly human education. His pupil and rival Aristotle was less given to poetic flights, as far as we can determine from the lecture notes that have survived, but for him, too, freedom was the unimpeded capacity of a creature to make real the fulfillment that is built into its very nature. For man, that meant the attainment of practical and intellectual virtue: to contemplate what is good and to act in accord with it. The brave Stoic Epictetus boasted that no one could put fetters upon him. What enslaves us is not the will of another but our own will when we turn to vice. When Boethius was in prison, awaiting execution on a charge of treason trumped up by his political, religious, and cultural enemies, Lady Philosophy came to console him and to remind him that only he had the power to wander away from the true path.

I seek in this book to echo those voices as I look at how we raise our children. But I caution the reader. Those voices also warn us that virtue is difficult, hard-won. If freedom is a virtue, and if Dostoyevsky's Grand Inquisitor is right in saying that most people flee in terror from freedom, then you may wish to raise up Contented Cows, placidly chewing their cuds in a field of creature comforts, or Harried Hamsters, racing on the Mill of the World. If so, you, too, can read this book for profit. I will show you ten ways in which we are raising up people who enjoy a certain political license (though even that is starting to rasp our wrists and ankles) but who have all the genuine spiritual liberty of an opium addict. The chains are right here, if you like.

Yet so is the window.

1

Courses in Compulsion

The School

Picture the scene.

It's Norway, many centuries ago. A young man named Olav, when he was hardly more than a boy, fled from his homestead because of a manslaughter he committed in a drunken brawl, cleaving a man's back with an ax before the man could run him through with a sword. God had not yet sent down upon sinful mankind the eleventh plague of Egypt, the lawyers—creatures that have their place but that, in great numbers, are far more destructive than grasshoppers and frogs. So Olav could not immediately plead self-defense. He had to betake himself to the protection of a powerful earl and fight his battles, leaving his betrothed wife behind. And in those years he was gone from home, she, beautiful, sweet, inattentive, and sometimes weak of will, allowed a hearty young Icelander, partly by force, to take her in bed. The result is a small child, Eirik, whom Olav has adopted as his own, for his wife's sake.

He tries to love the boy. That is hard for him to do when the mother is near, because she spoils the child, but when father and stepson are outdoors, things are different:

They agreed much better when they were alone together. Eirik was then more obedient and less restless, and even if he was too fond of asking odd questions, there was often some sense in them. He swallowed every word from his father's lips with eyes and ears, and this made him forget to come out with his fables and rigmaroles. Without being himself aware of it, Olav was warmed by the affection the child showed him; he forgot his dislike of other days and let himself be warmed whenever anyone showed him the friendship which he found it so hard to seek for himself. So he met Eirik halfway with calm goodwill; he instructed the boy in the use of weapons and implements, which were still more like playthings, smiled a little at Eirik's eager questions and chatted with him as a good father talks to his little son.

Best of all for the little boy are the times when they go out in a boat, father and son, to fish with a hand line. Eirik rushes back into the house at night and gabbles on in a splash of words about all he learned from his father, about rowing and fishing and making knots and splicing ropes, and how pretty soon he'll be going along with his father and the other men to fish and to hunt in earnest. It's a wild exaggeration, born from the boy's need to be loved by the man he thinks is his true father. Yet in it, even in these less-than-ideal circumstances, we see that what the boy learns from Olav is somehow different from what he might have learned from anybody else or on his own. It is a fully human kind of learning, mingled with the liberating bonds of filial love and fatherly duty. It is a learning that enters the sanctum of the heart. The boy will no more forget it than he could forget his name.

That passage is from Sigrid Undset's *The Master of Hestviken*. Does it matter that it is a work of fiction? Undset lived in her beloved Norway until the invading Nazis forced her to flee for her life with one of her two sons, over the mountains into Sweden and then, by one risky stage after another, to America. The other son fell in battle in the first few weeks of fighting. Norway then was far more literate than America is now. Yet to live in a land so often buried under snow and darkened by the long winters, you have to know how to do many things. You have to know how to take care of large animals like sheep and cows; how to fish through the ice; how to use skis to travel long distances (as, for example, over the mountains into Sweden, to escape the Nazis); where to find bilberries and lingonberries and how to preserve them; how to cut down trees and hew the wood into planks for houses and sheds; how to bake, how to use a smokehouse for fish and bacon, how to mend frayed clothes, how to brew small beer and cider, and many other things that Undset describes with intelligence and care.

In other words, you have to learn. It is one of the great things that families are for.

Picture another scene.

It's a boat, off the Grand Banks of Newfoundland. Aboard are the captain, his teenage son, a couple of other fishermen, and a new arrival, a teenage boy named Harvey. How, you may ask, can somebody show up one night on a boat that is a hundred miles out to sea? By the good grace of God. The boy, vain, boastful, and useless, was traveling with his mother on a cruise ship to Europe when the seas got foggy and choppy and he turned green in the gills. Going up to the main deck, he leaned overboard to be sick and a great wave swept him off the deck and knocked him unconscious into the sea. There he was picked up by one of the boats belonging to the fishing crew.

And, since these are times before cell phones, that's where he's going to remain for several months before they put to shore again.

Nobody on a fishing boat can be idle weight. Here is Harvey being instructed with rough-and-ready courtesy by one of the fishermen. He is literally *learning the ropes*—that is, learning which rope hoists which sail or turns which boom:

> For an hour Long Jack walked his prey up and down, teaching, as he said, "things at the sea that ivry man must know, blind, dhrunk, or asleep." There is not much gear to a seventy-ton schooner with a stump-foremast, but Long Jack had a gift of expression. When he wished to draw Harvey's attention to the peak halyards, he dug his knuckles into the back of the boy's

neck and kept him at gaze for half a minute. He emphasized the difference between fore and aft generally by rubbing Harvey's nose along a few feet of the boom, and the lead of each rope was fixed in Harvey's mind by the end of the rope itself.

Then another one of the crew, a fellow named Tom Platt, gets in on the instruction, chattering about sails and spars that he used to handle on his old ship, the *Ohio*. The men compete with one another on how best to instruct the lad:

> "He'll be ruined for life, beginnin' on a fore-an'-after this way," Tom Platt pleaded. "Give him a chance to know a few leadin' principles. Sailin's an art, Harvey, as I'd show you if I had ye in the fore-top o' the—"
>
> "I know ut. Ye'd talk him dead an' cowld. Silence, Tom Platt! Now, after all I've said, how'd you reef the foresail, Harve? Take your time answerin'."
>
> "Haul that in," said Harvey, pointing to leeward.
>
> "Fwhat? The North Atlantuc?"
>
> "No, the boom. Then run that rope you showed me back there—"
>
> "That's no way," Tom Platt put in.
>
> "Quiet! He's l'arnin', an' has not got the names good yet. Go on, Harve."
>
> "Oh, it's the reef-pennant. I'd hook the tackle on to the reef-pennant, and then let down—"
>
> "Lower the sail, child! Lower!" said Tom Platt, in a professional agony.
>
> "Lower the throat- and peak-halyards," Harvey went on. Those names stuck in his head.

It's a gently comic situation, but the author of *Captains Coura-geous*, Rudyard Kipling, is showing us some interesting things about l'arnin'. The schooner is the school. The sailors, with their extravagant accents, their wild experiences, their salty language, their long-loved songs, and their bluff willingness to work with and for one another—for otherwise no schooner could ever leave the docks—are the instructors. The boy Harvey is the student. The proving grounds are the vast and dangerous waters of the North Atlantic.

And here someone raises a hand in objection. "Think of the ropes on the boat—excuse me, the schooner! Think of the routine, day in and day out! Think of the hours upon hours of scaling fish and salting them and packing them in barrels. How can you possibly consider it a life of freedom rather than compulsion?"

There is nothing so grand, so dangerous, so man making, as months out on the open sea, fishing for cod and relying on nothing but your wits, your strength, and the wits and strength of your fellow sailors. Sure, there's a routine, as there's a routine in the work of the farmer who wakes up with the roosters to tend to his cows, and a routine in the work of monks who rise before dawn to sing praises to God. But these routines are in harmony with the nature of things: with animals, with the sea, with the sun, and with the human spirit lifting itself up in praise. They are not compulsions of impotence. Think of them as the ropes on the schooner. Unless you have those ropes, and people who have "learned the ropes," as the nautical saying goes, that salty and dangerous experience would never be possible; the schooner could never leave the dock. The ropes raise the sails and let you catch the wind.

Yet the most important feature of the scene is not technological. We all understand that it would be a poor substitute if Harvey had been given a set of diagrams and told to study them. It would also be a poor substitute if Harvey had been shown around the schooner by a robot, intoning in a metallic drone, "This is the reef-pennant. These are the peak-halyards." For one thing, Harvey would lack the mnemonic reminders that Long Jack imparts to him with such effectual physicality. He would never feel the ends of the booms rasping against his nose, or the free end of a rope thwacking him on the shoulders, or human knuckles burrowing into the back of his neck.

But even those reminders would not really do good work if they were not salted with the affection that the older men clearly show for the kid, as is shown by Jack's calling him Harve for short. A human being is meant to be taught by human beings for human things. That can never be accomplished by mere methods.

Think of any real encounter with another human mind and heart. Think of a small boy sitting on the knee of his grandfather, looking into his face and listening to how he once went barnstorming through Italy, earning his bread and oil and a dry bed by playing baseball for Italians who had never seen the game. Such a man was my friend, distantly related to Abe Lincoln, who would have appreciated the jaunt, being something of a river rat himself. Who is such a fool as to suggest that the child would do better to skitter through the Internet, with the keyword "Italy"? The real complexity of that encounter makes the screen, for all its technological intricacy, look like a stone knife or a pointed stick. But the encounter's worth abounds far above the complexity. It stirs in the heart. It is mingled with love and admiration. It declares, "This was a *good* thing to do!"

Even a dog cannot be well trained without affection. Dogs, we know, cannot just be inserted into the gaps of a contentment machine for wealthy professionals. Dogs need fresh air, exercise, play, the adventure of the pack. They should not be kenneled up all day.

Now look at how we treat children. They are kenneled up nine months of the year, institutionalized ten hours a day. We persist in believing that children, *because* they are intelligent, are more malleable than dogs. Notice the word taken from metallurgy. We will not see that it is just because they *are* intelligent that their teaching can never be training and can never subordinate the personal to the mechanical. They need to learn more than the rules. They need to learn the ropes. They need to do more than learn laws. They need to be inspired to loyalty. They need the adventure of love.

Harvey has that adventure, as the captain becomes a new father to him. Because he learns, he can go out one day with his pal on a rowboat fishing on their own. Because he learns, he grows so well into manhood that, when he finally meets his father on land again, he can speak to him frankly and sensibly about his future. He is no longer a silly spoiled brat. He has grown into freedom.

An Interminable Ride to a Terminal Place

And now, a different manner of conveyance.

"Imagine," said my friend, "how long it takes the bus to go from Little Anse," a village at the extreme end of the island where my family and I spend our summers, "all the way out to the Academy, stopping every five hundred feet."

"It must take an hour at least."

"Try an hour and a half, twice a day."

The people of Little Anse and the two neighboring villages are fierce defenders of their local church, St. Joseph's, where Masses have been said for many decades in French. They are determined that, if one or two of the four churches on the island must close, it won't be theirs. But the English speakers among them no longer have a school to defend with that same determination. The Academy, as the high school is called, is, like most such institutions in the United States and Canada, in the middle of nowhere, inaccessible except by bus and set far from the road so as to discourage casual visitors.

Why do people invariably enjoy visiting old one-room schoolhouses? I think it's because they are human places, on a human scale, for the education of little human beings. It isn't just that one knows, without having to think about it consciously, that the planks and joists were pegged together by the hands of the same people whose children would go to school there. It's that the whole *idea* of the school was founded upon natural desires and intentions.

There's the boiler, to keep the class warm in winter. There's the woodshed for the boiler. The men would stock that shed, and boys would haul the logs in when needed. There's the schoolyard, cleared for play. There are the windows, for natural light and for fresh air when the spring comes. There's the American flag, and a portrait of Washington, Father of the Country, or the Canadian flag, and a portrait of Queen Victoria. There are the books, tailored for children, certainly, but also compact, without wasted space—books were expensive. The readers are filled with folktales and poems and historical fiction and, for the older children, selections from Cicero, Shakespeare, Milton, and Pope.

The school looks in part like a home, or a small town hall, or a chapel. Appropriately so, since it is a public extension of the home, in harmony with the virtues encouraged by the church. As at home, as in church, children intermingle, the older ones seeing to the younger ones. There is no unnatural separation by year of birth. The teacher is hired by the people, for their purposes; he or she is not a member of a cabal intent upon subverting the purposes of their employers. The school belongs to the people who live there. It is their free and liberty-making creation.

Such schools, or schools somewhat larger but similar, used to be everywhere. One of my earliest memories is of a wooden schoolhouse painted blue, not five hundred feet from our back door. One night we saw it burning to the ground. My mother went there when she was a little girl. When she was older, she walked to the small high school "downtown," a little less than half a mile away. That structure, next to the rectory and the Catholic church and across the street from the parish hall, the Knights of Columbus, a candy store, and a barbershop, met its fate around 1970, when three towns consolidated into one district and built a new high school, sprawling, expensive, ugly, and inaccessible. The last time the building was used was as a home base for the town's centennial celebration in 1976. It remained boarded up for years, till it was condemned and torn down. Now a little park and garden commemorate where the high school—where my mother learned Latin, in a graduating class of about thirty—*used to be.*

For a long time, the poison of compulsion was kept in check by poverty. People simply couldn't afford to destroy the natural institution to benefit the unnatural. There was no way to whisk hundreds of children miles away to the impersonal Academy, built by contractors and staffed by people largely unknown and with purposes of their own, for whom parents are either compliant clients, no-shows, or pests. So, even though it was made compulsory for children to attend school, the compulsion had not yet begun to characterize the kind of school they were to attend. Victor Hugo's heroic revolutionary Enjolras, in *Les Misérables*, could call for "free and compulsory" schooling, without any sense of irony or paradox. But that state of affairs could not last.

It did not survive the revolution in transportation that replaced legs with wheels. Let us think about this for a minute. Sometimes things that are right in our path are the last things we see.

The school bus and the school warehouse go together. The latter requires the former. The school bus and the school as an institution set over *against* the family and family loyalties also go together. The former makes possible the latter. One hulk of an institution is not the same thing as ten schools put together. It is ten schools obliterated, with a hulk, a thing of a different sort, to take their place.

The child walks to the small school nearby. The connection between home and the school is felt in the soles of his feet. It's not just the place to which he is shipped, in garish yellow locomotive boxes. It's the place where he *goes*. It may still be a bad place—more on that soon. But it is a place involved with all the other places nearby and along the way. The child takes a different route home and stops in at the pharmacy to buy a comic book. He passes by a friend trudging up his front steps and says, "See you tomorrow." He climbs a hill bordering on some woods and sees a snapping turtle sunning himself on a rock. He stops, in the immemorial way of boys everywhere, to poke at the turtle with a stick to see if he snaps or ducks inside his shell.

Multiply this child by the other boys and girls in the school. On every street around the school, within the radius of a half hour's walk, there are boys and girls, big and small, mostly in knots of four and five but sometimes alone, trudging, lugging books over the shoulder or in bags, sometimes running, and sometimes already playing before they've gone home to change their clothes.

Let us sever the natural connection and forge an artificial one. And let us add to it the flair of dull repetition.

Charlie Chaplin is working on an assembly line. He tightens bolts with a pair of wrenches. He does this without stop, over and over, hours on end. The repetitive motion drives him temporarily mad: the machine takes over the man. He leaves the factory with the wrenches still in his hands, trying to "tighten" everything in sight that looks like a pair of bolts, including the buttons on the breasts of a woman's dress. That invasion of the machine *into* him is like what happens when, by accident, he is sucked into the works of the machine, and we see the little mustachioed fellow cranked this way and that between the thing's gigantic gears and cables.

Perhaps the people who run our schools should check out a copy of *Modern Times* and consider the nifty Billows Feeding Machine, to which Charlie is strapped for automatic lunch, with mechanical arms to give him his soup and wipe his mouth. The genius of the Billows Feeding Machine is efficiency. Why should the human cog take thirty minutes for lunch when he can take ten? That's twenty minutes saved for work, and time is money. Students who have an hour for lunch rather than a few rushed minutes may get into trouble, it's often said. At that I throw my hands up in despair and cry, "Better human trouble than inhuman order!"

The school has become the Billows Teaching Machine. We're so accustomed to its ways that we can scarcely imagine any alternative. Children *must* be segregated by age. Why? Is that natural? Do all children learn the same things at the same time and the same rate? Uniformity is the product of a machine, not of a living organism, much less the living spiritual being called man. Children *must* be hustled from room to room, or from subject to subject, at the ringing of a bell. Why? Do all subjects that merit study fit neatly into forty-two-minute cubbyholes? What if a child's interest in the subject is just beginning to kindle? Doesn't that matter? What if it just takes longer to read a chapter of *Treasure Island*? Should the child have to curtail the reading in midevent—freezing Jim Hawkins in the apple barrel or Israel Hands on the mizzen, with a knife in his teeth and murder in his heart?

I know, I know, I am a college professor. I, too, meet my students at a certain time, for an hour, and then time is up (though we don't have bells, and though, late in the afternoon, I'll often ask my students to stick around a little longer). We take it all for granted. Why? And the always somewhat arbitrary division of the day into subjects—why?

Homeschoolers know what I am getting at here. When Socrates and Phaedrus were sitting under the plane tree on the country road from Athens, no bell rang to tell the old man it was time to move from moral philosophy to metaphysics. "Sorry, Phaedrus, but your time is up"—no one can imagine Socrates saying such a thing. When Jesus sat upon the hillside and taught the crowds, he and they were so taken up into meditation upon the kingdom of God that they lost all sense of time, and soon the sun was setting and—well, unless you are a reader of the *New York Times* or a graduate of Harvard, you know the rest of the story.

When, in *Paradise Lost*, Adam and Eve are sitting in the cool of the evening, recalling when they first met and praising the goodness of God, Eve expresses a joy that teachers and students should know but rarely have the chance to know: "With thee conversing I forget all time; / All seasons, and their change, all please alike." That was, of course, when people measured their works according to the place of the sun and the state of the weather; the whole world was their time. That whole world had not yet been concentrated into the electric clicks of a machine on a wall.

Stannous Humanide

The chief lesson that the bell teaches is that all things must serve a utilitarian purpose. I recall reading in the *Princeton Alumni Weekly*, an insufferable publication of my *mater avaritiae*, about how a certain alumna managed time with her small boy. He was allowed to approach the Presence between three and three thirty, but then he had to leave, because Mummy had *important work* to do, evidently far more important than was the small boy. But also more important than Mummy. The bell says, "Nothing is of ultimate concern, because all things end when I determine." There are only two reasons why one would study a thing that is not of ultimate concern or that does not bring delight that carries us out of ourselves, as experiences of love and beauty do. One is that it is *useful*, a means to a farther end. The other is that we have no choice. We are *compelled* to do it. And since the experience of love or of beauty is by its nature impossible to compel, any justification for the compulsion must rest on utilitarian grounds. But that reduces education to a tool, and a tool that is often of dubious quality.

Predictably so, since the children themselves are treated as tools of dubious quality. They are treated as advance troops in remaking the human material known as their parents. They are educated not as persons made in the image and likeness of the living God but as pawns in a sociopolitical game; they are valued not in themselves and for themselves but for what they will accomplish. They will be rewarded according to how well they adapt themselves to the Teaching Machine, whose judgments are at once lax (for the Machine does not actually teach a great lot) and severe (for the judgments enter the Book of Life, with implications for college and employment thereafter, worldliness without end).

And thus it is that the purpose of the Machine is to instill the social-antisocial. Employers prize college graduates not for their knowledge, which is often scanty, but for their having exhibited a certain compliance and adaptation to routine. Does Number 1728 show up for work on time? Does he—or she, or it—know how to follow instructions? Can we trust it to speak more or less plainly on a telephone? Will its memos be marginally readable?

The salesmen of the Teaching Machine, aware that children who are whisked out of their control usually learn quite a lot that is never taught within the Machine, fall back upon an impregnable defense.

Then it is that we learn what the Machine is for. It is not for teaching children but for *socializing them*. Notice the ugly word, as if it were describing a chemical process for transforming worthless dross into something useful, like a rubber tire. *Socializing* evidently does not mean that the Teaching Machine imparts the difficult virtues of courage, temperance, prudence, and justice, much less such family-building and family-protecting virtues as manliness, womanliness, and chastity. Those virtues set a people free. But we do not want a free people. Free people are not predictable. We want a *managed* people.

So we teach them how to sit still, how to obey bells, how to make insipid clichés pass for thought, how to be "subversive" in trivial and uniform ways, how to think "outside the box" of tradition and wisdom and into the stainless steel cage of the politically "correct," how to extend the political pinky while sipping the political tea. The Teaching Machine serves as a Sanding, Veneering, and Finishing School for people who will work at moving memoranda from shelf A to shelf B (if they are good students and well socialized) or at moving potato product from bag C to trough of boiling fat D (if they are not good students but are still well socialized). Meanwhile, the school is so large that it must, for most students at most times, be essentially anonymous—no one knows everyone, and no one comes close; everyone every day passes by faces he cannot identify and never will identify. The school is a pit of backbiting, tale bearing, vindictiveness, cruelty, snobbery, fear, ambition, flattery, and hard-heartedness.

The Machine That Serves the Teaching Machine

When he was governor of Maine, Angus King made sure that there was a computer on the desk of every middle-school child in the state. I am, of course, writing this book on a computer. I'm not entirely happy about that. But it's a machine; I use it, I put it away—or try to put it away. Sometimes I have to make a vow to put it away, because the quick gratification that the online world provides—click!—is addictive. We all know this. No pretending that it isn't.

The computer is a symbol of what modern education has become and a diagnostic sign of our severely depleted souls. For the modern educator, and many people who consider themselves conservative will agree with this, education is a problem of *techne*: it is technological, in the broadest sense. I don't mean that it employs tools. I mean that it submits to them. The child is a problem that needs to be solved, a variable that needs to be settled, a vessel that needs to be filled, a connection that needs to be forged. How do we give children the *information* they need? Or what *methods* can we use to ensure "student learning objectives" or whatever the techno-lingo is?

What *skills*—notice the word imported from manual labor—must we build up in them so that they may *succeed* in the world? Notice, *succeed*: a plank succeeds if it holds up the porch; a winch succeeds if it lifts the stone; a commercial succeeds if it brings in a certain profit.

But human beings are not riverbeds for pile drivers to sink concrete piers into. Data are not information; information is not knowledge; and knowledge is not wisdom. What is the difference between the computer and a good book? One could, I suppose, read *Captains Courageous* from a computer screen. I doubt it. One might zip through the pages. But the book, no doubt, is the most sophisticated and *human* tool we have ever produced. I hold it in my hand. I turn its pages. I see its drama portrayed in ink illustrations here and there. I have memories of words, memories that are visual, auditory, and tactile. I can set it down for a moment and think. I can pick it up again later. I can read the last chapter over again. I can read the whole book over again. In its words the mind of a man, his personality, his thoughts, his manner of expression, his view of the world, enter my own mind—not as a commercial battering against my ears but as a friend, with an arm round my shoulder.

I take *Captains Courageous* with me. The book does not have to be plugged in, only opened. Or closed—I take it with me that way, too.

I walk down to the big swampy pond a few blocks away and look at the fish darting about, and I think of Disko Troop and his jocular son and the once-spoilt Harvey, with the seawater sloshing over the gunwales, while nets full of cod are emptied aboard and the fish packed in the hold, hours and hours through the cold night. The book is a companion. Rudyard Kipling, dead long ago, is not dead but speaks to me, even when I am but walking down the path. The words of the tale, artfully constructed, read in blessed solitude, enter my thoughts like the undertone of a song. I say, "I wish I had been that lad, fishing off the Grand Banks, working like a horse and sleeping like a dead man." No movie can do the same, especially not when "special effects" ruin our slender opportunities to attend to a face, a gesture, or a word.

What about the inescapable computer, that costly thing on the student's desk in "good" schools? It scratches the itch for instant "information" at the expense of knowledge and wisdom. That itch was there in schools even before the computer came along to scratch it, but the machine has caused that same compulsion to spread like a rash over the body of the usual curriculum.

I have witnessed a change in college, too. My students and I were recently discussing Romano Guardini's *The End of the Modern World*. Modern man, says Guardini, was characterized by an often naive trust in the inevitable emancipation to be gained by means of machines. One man with a backhoe can dig a trench in a day that it would have taken twenty men at least as long to dig, and with much sweat and strained muscles. But our love for our machines has grown deeply ambivalent, and sometimes we feel powerless to resist them. The servants have become our masters. Machines have intruded where they do not belong, not to enhance a man's muscle but to replace his thought and deaden his heart. So they tell me of lecturers who now use only screens and visual presentations, which means that all of their thought is necessarily reduced to what can conveniently be presented, with bullet points and pictures and easy captions and graphs. There are now teachers who would be utterly lost—at sea, and lacking the long experience of Disko Troop—without the machine.

Can it impart a list of items to be copied? Yes, certainly. Can it teach a human being? No, not unless we conceive the human being as a machine, like a container for data or a grinder and processor of citations. No real man ever wooed a woman with a prospectus.

No Matter How Bad You Think It Is

It's worse.

I have been describing how and where our children are taught. I have not yet touched upon *what* they are taught.

Chasing after truth is to a child's mind what good food and fresh air and exercise are to a child's body. It makes the mind strong and supple. But the purpose of the chase is the catch, and a strong mind enjoying a perceived truth is ready to flex its muscles and find more. Or, to change the metaphor, every perceived truth is like a lens or an eye. It is light that brings more light. This is true of matters of fact but far truer of matters of value: of goodness and beauty. A good poet sweats and strains for the grand effect. A great poet seems to find the right word without any effort at all. He is the master of his words; the bad poet is their flunky. A man trained up in the virtue of courage sees many possibilities when the cannons of the enemy come trundling up the ridge; the coward thinks only of flight.

Virtue liberates; vice enslaves. A passion for genuine beauty liberates; to submit to the ugly, the drab, the slipshod, and the squalid is to give up the noble journey. It is to leave the pilgrimage and agree to be a subject of those who have never taken up the pilgrimage, or those who have failed likewise, or those who hate beauty itself. A passion for goodness—not niceness, not political etiquette—liberates; to submit to the venal, the self-indulgent, the wanton, the mendacious, is to agree to be bound by lies.

Edmund Spenser gives us a remarkable allegorical vision of the difference between the steadfastness of virtue and the fixity of vice. His still-naive hero, Red Cross Knight, a bit too confident of his own powers, has recklessly entered the den of the monster Error, against the urging of the chaste maiden Una, whom he loves and whom he has sworn to assist, in ridding her parents' realm of the dragon that has held them bound. But Error, a dragon herself, with ferocious claws and a long deadly tail wound up in knots and tangles, does something that Red Cross Knight should have expected, after he has wounded her:

> Much daunted with that dint, her sense was dazed,
>> Yet kindling rage, herself she gathered round,
>> And all at once her beastly body raised
>> With doubled forces high above the ground:
>> Then wrapping up her wreathèd stern around,
>> Leapt fierce upon his shield, and her huge train
>> All suddenly about his body wound,
>> That hand or foot to stir he strove in vain:
> God help the man so wrapped in Error's endless train.

Una will cry out, "Add faith unto your force, and be not faint," inspiring Red Cross with the strength to strangle Error before the monster strangles him. But we should look closely at his predicament here, which will serve as an emblem of vice in general, both intellectual and moral.

The Knight is bound by Error, the form of whose body suggests both imprisonment and wandering: her very name, Error, means to stray, to wander from the right path. Her "train" is "endless," meaning that it seems to go on forever but also that it has no end, no goal, no purpose. It is therefore at once a stunning picture of aimless wandering and of fixity, of traveling on and on in no right direction and of being bound so tight that you cannot stir a hand or a foot.

Red Cross will wriggle out of this threat, but he will fall to the next, persuaded by a wicked purveyor of false images that Una has been unfaithful to him. His straying, paradoxically and appropriately, lands him in a couple of prisons, while Una wanders over the land in search of him. He has erred; he has strayed from truth; he seems to be following his own will, but that is imprisonment. He is in dread danger of collapsing into what Milton, taught well by his predecessor, attributes to Satan, who boasts of his *fixed mind*. Una searches everywhere; she has not strayed, because she loves him still. She is steadfast even though she travels many a mile.

C. S. Lewis, following in the steps of both Spenser and Milton— and Dante, and Scripture—gives us a scene in *That Hideous Strength* that well illustrates the principle. The intellectual villain Wither, suddenly made aware of the imminent downfall of the evil tangle of compulsions to which he has given his soul, cannot do anything other than what he has already done. He is aware, as a theoretical possibility, that he *could* repent. But he no longer has the will to repent, even if it should require no more of him than the slightest movement, such as would suffice to brush a fly from his arm. He suffers the consequences of his intellectual evil. He believed in determinism, and that has robbed him of his freedom. Believe in chains that do not exist: your belief in the chains will bind you.

So our schools instruct young people to believe in chains.

Everywhere we turn, we find the chains. I am not speaking here about the lineaments of human nature—of the boundaries, like skin, that make us the kind of beings we are. When we recognize those lineaments, they, too, are liberating. We deny them at peril of imprisonment in phantasms. I am speaking here about insidious kinds of determinism, preached to our students so as to give them the illusion of mastery.

One kind of determinism is bound up with the urge to cram everything we study into certain approved pigeonholes. If we are to know a human being, we should not begin with race or class or "gender," that category invented by social critics who avert their eyes, prim and prying at once, from the frank and plain reality of sex. We certainly cannot end there. If I say, "Who is John?" you cannot answer me correctly by saying that he is six feet tall, 150 pounds, with Italian and Irish ancestry on his mother's side and African American and Latino ancestry on his father's side, with a family income of such and such a year, voting in such a pattern, living on Maple Street and selling insurance. These are all *things about* John, but they are not John, the man. It does violence to the man to reduce him to such categories. It is an act of contempt for his humanity. It reduces him, not so that we may get to know him, *but so that we can manipulate facts about him while not getting to know him at all*. It is a study in subhumanity.

That is exactly what schoolteachers and professors do to *John's art* when they reduce it the categories of race, class, and gender.

I recall here an incident that occurred at my generally healthy college several years ago. I and my teammate in the theology department were teaching one of the freshman sections of our course in the Development of Western Civilization. A young lady approached us one day in tears. She had enrolled, not knowing what she was getting into, in Introduction to Women's Studies, taught by an art professor who could speak of nothing but race, class, and gender. The material for that course was the fairy tale. When they got round to the story she loved the most when she was a little girl, "Beauty and the Beast," and finished reducing it to the standard patriarchal conspiracy against the development of women—despite the fact, which should be obvious to the most inattentive reader, that Beauty is the dominant character in what is essentially a story of praise for the power of a good and strong woman—the student could not take it anymore. She approached my colleague and me and asked what to do. We told her to stick it out, but she dropped the class, prompting an aggressive campaign by the feminist professor against my colleague two years later when he was up for a promotion.

Why read at all if you are not going to accept the work on its own terms? Criticism becomes nothing more than an imposition of the self upon the poet and his art. The poet does not teach us; we teach the poet. We ply our "theory" upon a poet who cannot answer back. We dress it with pseudo-scientific language to impress the sophomores while remaining impervious to the poet's thought and his humanity. This is called "critical thinking," quite uncritical about itself and predictable in its results, as if a living being were pressed through a grinder.

Such reduction is not only violent. It is *stupid*. It misses the point. How does one read of a sinful man's falling to his knees to beg forgiveness of the girl he had attempted to murder when she was an infant and not notice the resurrection of a human soul, but instead declare that Shakespeare's *Tempest* is *really* about colonies (there are no colonies in the play) in the New World (it's in the Mediterranean), established by men of adventure (the protagonist was shipwrecked and is trying to get back home) to make their fortune (he will bring back nothing)?

Another kind of determinism is bound up with the denial of virtue itself. A student will hear that Homer made his heroine Penelope steadfast in marriage because *that was the expectation given to him by his culture*. Homer, then, is boxed up and bound. He *had to be that way*, because of when and where he lived. Here again, reduction. A student will hear that Shakespeare cast doubt upon Juliet's passion and her disobedience to her father because people believed such things then; Shakespeare *had to be that way*. Besides being an offense to these brilliant poets, such chatter leads nowhere. It is like wandering inside a corral. The students do not ask, "Was Homer right?" or "What does Shakespeare see that I might not see?" They are encouraged to stand over and against Homer and Shakespeare, not seeing that the determinism by which they misjudge those poets will bind them hand and foot. For the corollary to the lie that Shakespeare had to be that way is that *we have to be this way*. If those great minds were no other than the sum of forces of cultural influence, then we too, whose minds are not so great, will be no otherwise. If gold is mud, we need not talk about iron—or rust.

A related kind of determinism is bound up with the denial of beauty. Students hear that beauty is what a culture determines it to be, and nothing else. They are not taught the difference between a subjective experience of something real and an imaginary construct of a subjective experience. I look upon Rembrandt's painting *The Return of the Prodigal Son* and see the kindly old father leaning over his kneeling son, his hands upon the boy's back, old hands, gnarled, fleshy, gentle, infinitely patient. My experience of those hands is subjective: I cannot reduce it to a formula to be replicated in bottles of artistic appreciation, labeled and sold at museums everywhere. But what I experience subjectively is real: the beauty *is there.*

How terrible is the denial of beauty! If students hear that there is no real difference between the artistic perfection of Tennyson's *The Lotos-Eaters* and the latest bit of doggerel by a mass-marketed popular musician, they will fall back into the very spiritual and intellectual indolence and subhumanity that Tennyson's poem presents to us as a threat. The mariners of Odysseus have come ashore on the land of Lotus-eaters. They are weary. They want to give up the journey home. The Lotus is sweet; the Lotus allows you to forget; the Lotus brings soft chains:

> Surely, surely, slumber is more sweet than toil, the shore
> Than labour in the deep mid-ocean, wind and wave and oar;
> O, rest ye, brother mariners, we will not wander more.

They want to give up direction: the journey to where they ought to be. They want a life of no direction: to sit in the land of the Lotus-eaters and allow the waves of insignificance to wash over them and drift them here and there. If you are not in love with beauty and goodness, you will be clutched by the drab and the listless, if not worse. To say to young people, "There are no such things, really, as beauty and goodness," is to do far worse than to fail to direct them out of the cave and into the sun. It is to cut out the hearts of those who might still be minded to make that pilgrimage. It is worse than to fail to direct the ship of the soul by the constant star of the North. It is to tear the tiller out of the ship entirely and leave it at the mercy of the winds, and to call the aimlessness "freedom."

All of these things are soul-binding forms of nihilism, which in its somewhat feminine version shows up as an intolerant condemnation of anyone who makes any kind of judgment whatsoever. One must not "judge." I encountered this nihilism one day when I found myself in an argument with a student who insisted that all forms of judgment were merely relative to the society in which they were made, and that outside of that society we could not judge them at all. The position is self-contradictory, of course, because it is itself a judgment, one that is notably severe in its attack on the very principle of judgment. The student went so far as to insist that we could not stand in judgment over the men who murdered Jews in the gas chambers of Nazi Germany. "What was right for the Nazis was right for the Nazis," she said. This statement cannot be characterized as mere moral relativism. It was absolute dogma. It had to be upheld, even at the cost of justifying the monsters. It was an example of induced compulsion. *Thou shalt not say, "Thou shalt not!" Thou shalt not think.*

Plato traveled all the way to tyrant-ruled Syracuse in a failed attempt to revive in Greece a love for justice. Our schools teach the child who would be Plato that justice is only what we say it is, so he might as well stay put. Justice is only the will of the stronger, said the sophist Thrasymachus, against whose nihilism Plato committed his life. We say the same, but in more effeminate terms. Justice is only what a "culture," meaning a shifting majority of people, say it is, with a dollop of respect for "human rights" spread on top, without intellectual foundation, and without any connection with virtue and duty.

The angel struck Peter on the side, and the chains in his prison cell dropped from his hands. It is a vision of grace and freedom, of the gospel leaving behind the rough chains of a decadent world that knew only power. We prefer chains to that gospel.

2

Contempt for Humanity

The Corpse

In February 1910 the literary critic and philosopher Paul Elmer More came to the Women's Club of Saint Louis to speak about the value of the critical imagination in the present time.

Before I describe what he said, I'd like to note how far this event was from anything in our current experience. The Women's Club of Saint Louis still exists and still holds events in its lovely brownstone mansion, but it is now mainly a pleasant social club for older women, with a fine hall to rent for weddings and other celebrations. But it had been founded in 1904 to welcome families of foreign dignitaries arriving in Saint Louis for the World's Fair, and it was conceived as a club for the promotion of letters and the arts. Hence the invitation to More.

The editor of *The Essential Paul Elmer More*, Byron C. Lambert, says that More wrote the speech in a hurry. We should all be so adept at recalling, evaluating, and affirming on the run. To the women of Saint Louis, who—note well—had not yet received the franchise to vote, More spoke about the diary of quotations and short admonitions to himself that Matthew Arnold kept, published posthumously by his daughter in 1902. "I do not know to what work in English to liken it," says More at the beginning of his lecture to those daughters of the Gateway to the West, in that city of rivermen, cattlemen, farmers, brewers, and manufacturers, "unless it be the notebooks containing quotations from Marcus Aurelius and Epictetus written down by the author of the *Characteristics* with his comments, which Dr. Rand edited in 1900 as the *Philosophical Regimen of Anthony, Earl of Shaftesbury.*"

Utter that sentence anywhere in the English-speaking world now and you might as well be speaking Old Elvish to Eskimos.

More expected the women in his audience not only to know who Arnold and Shaftesbury were but also to appreciate the similarities between the morose apostle of culture and the more cheerful apostle of good breeding and generous morality. They were to follow him as he traced the intellectual lineage of Arnold and Shaftesbury back to Cicero, whom he praises for his balance and deep humanity. They were to have a feel for the sensibleness of Erasmus and the fiery monomania of Luther. They were to understand why Arnold called the reformer "a Philistine of genius," and not to be surprised when Cardinal Newman agreed with that estimate.

More expected them to appreciate, indeed to recall, a notorious attack made upon Arnold. Henry Sidgwick, disgusted by Arnold's recommendation for delay and deliberation when it came to social reform, derided the "Prophet of Culture" as a "cheerful modern liberal, tempered by renunciation, shuddering aloof from the rank exhalations of vulgar enthusiasm, and holding up the pouncet-box of culture betwixt the wind and his nobility." More expected his audience to understand and consider the converse, that even though Arnold had not gotten the whole matter right, having lost his religious faith and replaced it with faith in culture, his critical imagination was still as needful as ever.

It wasn't just that Paul Elmer More could drop forty or fifty names and expect recognition. His lecture dealt with a permanent moral and intellectual concern: How are we to bring together our love for the beautiful with our difficult and often disappointing devotion to what is morally right? Or, *how are we to be fully human?* He ranged over broad fields of thought and art. He spoke of philosophers ancient and modern—Plato and Descartes, Marcus Aurelius and Bergson. He spoke of the urbane man of letters and the passionate adherent to a single large truth, of Horace and Pascal, of Cicero and Saint Paul. He spoke of cultured skeptics like Renan and profoundly religious poets like Vaughan and, in his way, Wordsworth. He ranged over centuries and nations: in France with Rousseau and Sainte-Beuve; in Italy with Leopardi and Jacopone da Todi; in ancient Rome with Lucan and Lucretius; in Greece with Theocritus and Homer; in Victorian England with Ruskin and Carlyle, Huxley and Wilde; in America with Whitman and William James. The women in his audience, even if they could not all read Homer in the Greek, must have followed him well enough to make the lecture a success, because he gave it twice again, at Yale and at Columbia.

With what *freedom* did he speak!

And what did he say? We must not allow ourselves to be shackled to the past because it is past. But we do not win our freedom by ignoring the past because it is past. We win our freedom by using our critical imagination, which makes the past present to us, and makes us the heirs of a prodigious patrimony:

> We suffer not our individual destiny alone but the fates of humanity also. We are born into an inheritance of great emotions—into the unconquerable hopes and defeated fears of an immeasurable past, the tragedies and the comedies of love, the ardent aspirations of faith, the baffled questionings of evil, the huge laughter at facts, the deep-welling passion of peace. Without that common inheritance how inconceivably poor and shallow would be this life of the world and our life in it!

That makes us more than interesting guests at a tea party. We do more than smell the literary lilacs and lavender. We do *other* than hold a pouncet-box between the winds of suffering mankind and our noble education—and this is what the reforming Sidgwicks of the world do not grasp. We walk in the freedom of weighing things, valuing things, judging things.

We are set free to stand with Hector on the windy plains of Troy. We deliberate with the failed statesman Cicero, awaiting his brutal assassination at the hands of the henchmen of Mark Antony. We raise our cry with Job on the dunghill, we weep with Peter on that dreadful night in Jerusalem, we gaze in wonder with Augustine and Monica looking seaward at Ostia. Emily Dickinson was not indulging a flight of fancy when she said that the book is a noble chariot "that bears a human soul."

We mount that chariot by an active and creative memory. Without memory, truly human thought is impossible; we are left with mere reaction to impulses, which are to thought as slogans are to language. "We have all of us met now and then in our daily intercourse," said More, "a man whose conversation impressed us immediately as possessing a certain ripeness of wisdom, a certain pertinency and depth of meaning. If we wished to characterize such a man [with] a single word, we should perhaps say that he was essentially educated." He "moves forward, not at haphazard, but by the direction of some principle of conduct," and "can be depended upon for counsel and comfort."

The value of the old liberal education was not that it made men "well-rounded," like a ball bearing, but that it gave them the freedom of the height and breadth and depth of human experience, including man's mysterious encounter with his Creator. To be free is not to live in no place and at no time but to live in one place as in the shadow of all places, and to live in one time as in the morning twilight of eternity.

Dewey's Decimation

What happened to this freedom-making education? The short answer is that John Dewey happened to it.

Dewey, mild of temperament, was as narrow-minded a reformer as the world has ever been plagued withal. He was an atheist who employed the language of religiosity to advance the oldest of new new things, a worship of a certain form of political power. "Put not your trust in princes," says the wise old Psalmist. Dewey liked princes well enough, but what he really trusted was principality: the new lordship of the "people," democrats trained to do good work in the factories, to vote responsibly, to digest their food well and move their bowels once a day, to read the newspapers, and to follow the advice of their betters. These betters were the new priests, the scientists and social scientists: mostly what Russell Kirk called "philodoxers," lovers of utopian fantasies. Yet the most fantastical thing about Dewey and his followers was that they took their fantasies for the bald truth. They denied the very mainspring of fantasy, the human imagination, which is ultimately and incorrigibly religious. They did so as the acceptable price for banishing all the traditions and folkways that blocked the path of the progress they desired.

In this enterprise, Dewey had no sense of the value of the imagination as a truth-perceiving and truth-expressing faculty. He was what Arnold would have called a philistine with a hypertrophied brain. I have before me a copy of Dewey's seminal work *How We Think*. A signature on the inside cover reveals that it was owned by a woman named Miriam Hershey, in 1911, who was evidently studying under Dewey at the Teachers' College, Columbia University. From that college went forth missionaries of Dewey to all the so-called normal schools in the country—that is, the colleges that prepared the next generation of schoolteachers. The signature strikes me as a miraculously preserved fingerprint might strike a forensic detective at the scene of a crime, long unsolved.

Early in the book, Dewey is careful to distinguish between what qualifies as thought and what doesn't. The work of a child's imagination doesn't:

> The imaginative stories poured forth by children possess all degrees of internal congruity; some are disjointed, some are articulated. When connected, they simulate reflective thought;

indeed, they usually occur in minds of logical capacity. These imaginative enterprises often precede thinking of the close-knit type and prepare the way for it. But *they do not aim at knowledge, at belief about facts or in truths* [emphasis in the original]; and thereby they are marked off from reflective thought even when they most resemble it.

Miss Hershey has bracketed that passage as especially worthy of attention. The reader should note that Dewey does not dismiss the child's work because it is naive or childish. Everything that he says here can be applied also to Sophocles or Homer. It is the reduction of the category of truth to what a John Dewey might find comfortable. It is to employ the rules of the natural sciences beyond where they apply, and thus to rig the game from the beginning:

What is important, is that every inference shall be a tested inference; or (since often this is not possible) *that we shall discriminate between beliefs that rest upon tested evidence and those that do not, and shall be accordingly on our guard as to the kind and degree of assent yielded* [emphasis in the original].

In what I find to be a macabre irony, Miss Hershey has flagged the above as a "vital sentence," "to be remembered." Not the mighty strains of Milton singing "Of man's first disobedience, and the fruit / Of that forbidden tree," but the magisterial utterances of a man suffering an exaggerated case of intellectual myopia. In this entire work on human thought, the imagination appears only briefly, and never in its moral or spiritual capacity. It is only what we might call a practical curiosity, important in its limited sphere—the faculty whereby a child such as Edison might ask, "I wonder what would happen if I put oil on the saw before using it to cut wood?"

For a distinctively *human* imagination into human things, Dewey has no use. Dear reader, you may well remember the flights of inspiration you felt when you first heard of Odysseus or Jason or Odin, not to mention Moses before Pharaoh, or Jesus before Pilate. Dewey lets you know that that was only a case of nerves:

> Educators sometimes think children are reacting to a great moral or spiritual truth when the children's reactions are largely physical and sensational. Children have great powers of dramatic simulation, and their physical bearing may seem (to adults possessed with a philosophical theory) to indicate they have been impressed with some lesson of chivalry, devotion, or nobility, when the children themselves are occupied only with transitory physical excitations. To symbolize great truths far beyond the child's range of actual experience is an impossibility, and to attempt it is to invite love of momentary stimulation.

Dewey makes the point succinctly in a gloss on the side of the page: "*Only the already experienced can be symbolized*" (emphasis in the original).

In one stunningly obtuse sentence, Dewey has just dispensed with arts and letters almost entirely, to say nothing of religious faith and philosophy that rises above a worship of technology.

Hence we can deduce the movement to give to children living in slums stories about children living in slums, as "relevant," as "what they can relate to," or whatever the slang of our day is—but to admit the fancy only to the extent that it serves an approved political program.

According to Raymond Callahan, writing in *Education and the Cult of Efficiency*, John Dewey "stood almost alone in opposing the watering down of the curriculum," even though many people had "accused [him] of being responsible for the emphasis upon practical and immediately useful subjects." That meek defense notwithstanding, the "cult of efficiency" that Callahan rightly deplored was at one with the cult of technology and the reduction of thought to tool making that Dewey championed. Others may have built the machines; it was Dewey who taught a nation that machines were to be built. Shortly thereafter, America witnessed, at all the normal schools, an elevation of technique above mastery of the subject to be taught, and a loss of any sense of what a human education really is for. That problem was ably exposed a half century ago, by James Koerner in *The Miseducation of American Teachers*, and it is with us still.

Charles Darwin, late in life, wrote that poetry meant nothing to him. He had no ear for it, and he noted its loss with a mild regret. John Dewey had no poetry in his heart, and he never noticed the lack. He and his allies despised the old classical education that had marked the great private schools and that had exercised considerable influence upon the public schools. It was "dogmatic," they said, and the students learned "by rote." The slogans are still with us. So, too, the slander. *Something* impressive must have been imparted to those women in Saint Louis to enable them to join Paul Elmer More upon his mount of speculation. Even the worst of teachers cannot entirely smother the glory of a great dramatist. Let us take Aeschylus for example.

A boy is sitting beside his schoolmaster, plodding his way, after hours, through Aeschylus's *Agamemnon*. They are approaching the moment when Clytemnestra describes the welcome she gave to her long-departed husband, Agamemnon, upon his return from Troy. She had been harboring vengeance against him for ten years for his sacrifice of their daughter Iphigenia at the behest of the angry goddess Artemis. She has caught him in a net, literally, and while the man struggles in its coils, she stabs him again and again, slicking the floor of the palace with royal blood.

The boy is giving his translation, methodically, fitting every English noun and verb to every Greek noun and verb, to please the schoolmaster, who has, alas, failed in his long career to impart to the boys a love of the literature he teaches. All has been reduced to pedantry, to getting the cases and the tenses correct. There is more than one way to destroy a classic. Mr. Crocker-Harris is now known to the boys as the "Himmler of the Lower Fifth." No one likes him. All the boys flock instead to the classroom of Mr. Hunter, a good-looking young chemistry teacher who also, as it happens, is the lover of Crocker-Harris's wife. Science is more exciting than Greek, here. So is cricket.

But the boy, Taplow, suddenly shifts from grammar to human reality. "As she stood there in the gore of her dead husband," he says, abandoning the literal, his eyes growing wide with excitement and wonder.

The schoolmaster pauses to remove his spectacles. "I am impressed, Taplow," he says, "by your appreciation of the more lurid aspects of Greek drama," and he begs him to continue with a more literal translation. But Taplow resists. "Sir," he says, "it's a play, isn't it? And imagine, what a thing, for her to have murdered her husband and to say those words!"

Then the old schoolmaster, a failure, but a deeply human man for all that, reveals to Taplow that he, too, once translated the *Agamemnon*, or that he began to but never finished it. He translated it into rhyming couplets, he says, and adds that in one or two places he believed he had exceeded the original.

A permanent bond is being forged between the boy and the man. The scene is from Terence Rattigan's play and film *The Browning Version*. The student and his master are united by something that touches them in the depths of their souls. It is not just that Mr. Crocker-Harris, like Agamemnon, is bound to a shrewish wife. His love of Aeschylus was a youthful passion that preceded the unhappiness of his marriage. Crocker-Harris and Taplow are united by something that brings them wonder and that makes the science master's display of chemical explosion seem shallow and gimmicky by comparison.

I understand that I'm not being fair to the scientist, who also should address the world with patience and wonder, and whose discoveries have set many millions free from the drudgery of hard manual labor. And yet, and yet—the human things are deeper. A single toddling child kneeling to pick at the yellow fronds of a dandelion is a more astonishing thing, not least because he is capable of being astonished, than is that vast dead ball of gas we call Jupiter, and all its moons, and all its many storms. The problem comes when the tool masters the maker—when, as I have suggested, natural science devours the other disciplines, or when people who should have learned the mature judgments of the critical imagination cede pride of place to scientific methods that do not apply outside of their ambit.

Paul Elmer More saw this faddish idolizing of science at work in the departments of classics in his day. The professors devoted themselves to tracing the lineage of diphthongs, to reducing the ancient languages to systems amenable to quasi-mathematical analysis. They no longer were reading Homer for Homer. Meanwhile, from the other claw of the pincers came Dewey and the idolaters of a supposedly more "scientific" method of education, more democratic—that is, a method brazenly dismissive of the past and ready to toss away two thousand years of learning. More wrote in 1915, a hundred years ago, words that are even sadder to read now, as there are few people remaining who might understand them:

> The need is to restore to their predominance in the curriculum those studies that train the imagination, not, be it said, the imagination in its purely aesthetic function, though that aspect of it also has been sadly neglected, but the imagination in its power of grasping in a single firm vision, so to speak, the long course of human history and of distinguishing what is essential therein from what is ephemeral.

To dismiss the essential for the ephemeral is to introduce dementia into a nation or what remains of a culture. It is to embrace the "freedom" of an old man in a nursing home, staring at the lights and the noise from the television, able to carry on small talk for the nonce, to be moved by a commercial to desire better sealing wax, and to cheer or hiss at the political savior of the next fifteen minutes.

Dead Writing

Imagine a new father looking into the eyes of his child. A wisp of blond hair curls about the baby's scalp. The fingers, wrinkled like those of an old man, curl about his own finger. The child has blue eyes, but who knows whether they will stay that way? There's the slightest indentation in the chin, reflecting that of his wife, who cradles the baby in her arms and hums gently to him.

"Here is one," says the father, "who will be a productive member of the labor force, and who will assist in the increase of the Gross Domestic Product."

"Here is one," says the mother, "who will be adept at the processing of information, so as to facilitate the attainment of a successful career."

"Here is one," says the father, "who will possess the capacity to embark upon independent research, who will present arguments that balance claim and counterclaim."

"Here is one," says the mother, "who will meet the Common Core Requirement anchor standards and high school grade-specific standards, which work in tandem to define college and career-readiness expectations, the former providing broad standards, the latter providing additional specificity."

I did not make that last sentence up.

Quite a few bad ideas have plagued education in the United States since John Dewey and the application, en masse, of supposedly scientific methods to replace the slow and hard-won guidelines of the art of teaching. There was the New Math, essentially set theory for children, to tag with cumbersome names—the Commutative Property, the Distributive Property of Multiplication over Addition—what should have been natural and intuitive. There was the basal reader, an artificial timetable applied to the child's mind, whereby plenty of words were deliberately withheld from his eyes and utterly inane "stories" were cobbled together from a vocabulary too dull for a two-year-old: See John teach! Teach, John, teach!

There was the disastrous "Look and Say" method of teaching reading, which turned English words into Chinese pictograms and withheld from children the phonetics that would allow them to read words they had never seen before. There was the elimination of grammar from the curriculum, replaced by a scattering of rules for usage, many of them incorrect at that. There was the folding of history and geography into social studies, increasingly focused upon what was in the newspaper—the ephemeral. There was the abandonment of Latin and Greek in favor of modern languages, or no other languages at all, and the modern languages studied "conversationally," so that after four years of Spanish the typical high school senior will not be able to read a short story by Borges, much less *Don Quixote*. But that's all right, because he will be able to ask where the bathrooms are in Tijuana.

These and other follies share two features in common. They came trumped up with "science," and they were imposed upon an unwilling populace in the name of democracy. And they still come the same way. Behold, as the newest American example, the Common Core Standards in English Language Arts and Literacy in History/Social Studies, Science, and Technical Subjects.

There are so many bad things to say about these standards, one hardly knows where to begin. The field is full of rubble, and all I have here is a shovel and a small wheelbarrow. Still, one must begin somewhere. The standards are diagnostic of a persistent disease, so that what I say of these now will apply also to the next infection, whatever it may happen to be called.

The archons, like my monstrous imaginary parents above, forget that a child is a human being, not a data processor, not a lever in an economic machine, not a researcher piling up the articles and books for a sufficiently exhaustive bibliography, meaningless in itself. A child is a human being: and human beings are made in the image and likeness of God. That implies that the child is made for goodness and truth and beauty, and that he will respond to it, despite Dewey's absurd contempt for it and his reduction of their response to a case of the wiggles.

Every encounter with what is good—the chivalry of General Lee, the willing poverty of Mother Teresa, the shy greathearted youth of Alyosha Karamazov—can expand the soul; it helps to set us free from the compulsions of false goods, which Christians have long grouped under the headings of the seven deadly sins. Every encounter with beauty—the glint of a simple word in a poem by Herbert, the meditative subtleties of the late Shakespeare, the sweet charm of a ballad by Burns—can expand the soul; it helps to set us free from the heavy accretions of the drab, the dull, the mean, the spiritually sluggish, the smog of contemporary workaweek life. Every encounter with human truth—Jane Austen deftly showing how little we know our own motives; Dickens revealing the meaning of "economy" in the cheerful and charitable housekeeping of Esther Summerson, his finest heroine; or Shakespeare offering us the foolish Lear, mad and childish and yet "every inch a king"—can expand the soul; it helps to set us free from the common delusions of our time, the lies we believe and the lies we tell.

But the Common Core Standards in English Language Et Cetera know nothing of all this. For the archons, reading is a "skill," and that is that. *What* you read is of no import; only how complex the text is, judged according to various quantitative algorithms and a few subjective checklists that do not touch upon goodness, beauty, or truth.

That explains why the Common Core Standards jettison any systematic study of the history of English and American literature. It also explains why, as the children grow older, silly old poetry is progressively supplanted by "informational texts," Supreme Court opinions, newspaper editorials, and technical manuals. It explains the suffocating pseudoprofessional character of the writing that is required and praised.

Here, for example, is the opening of an essay that the keepers of the Common Core Standards uphold as exemplary for a high school senior. Allow me to boldface everything vague and abstract, and to italicize every irrelevant sentence:

The modern world *is full of* **problems and issues—disagreements** *between peoples that stem from* **today's wide array of perceptions, ideas, and values. Issues** *that could never have been* *foreseen are often identified and made known today because of* **technology**. *Once, there were scatterings of people who had the same idea, yet never took any action because none knew of the others; now, given our* **complex forms of modern communication**, *there are millions who have been connected. Today, when* **a new and arguable idea** *surfaces, the debate spreads across the* **global community** *like wildfire.* **Topics** *that the general public might never have become aware of are instantly made into news that can be discussed at the evening dinner table. One such matter, which has sparked the curiosity of millions, is* **the recent interest** *in* **the classification of literature as fiction or nonfiction**.

What's wrong with that writing? Everything. There are platitudes—dull and absurd at once, as if people are actually arguing about whether Ms. Opinionator is a fiction writer or just the usual editorial air machine. There's the wearisome and phony enthusiasm over "modern" this and "modern" that. The nouns are vague; *peoples* and *issues* are misused; *wildfire* is trite. And none of it is to the point.

But the real problem can't be cured by a visit to the English stylist. It's a problem that John Dewey was intelligent enough to recognize, if he had cared to, but that his descendants among us *cannot* recognize, just as a tone-deaf man cannot understand the beauty of the simple air that gives us Bach's *Jesu, Joy of Man's Desiring*. The real problem is not technical and is not primarily linguistic. It is human.

A human being wrote that passage, but not *as a human being*. He wrote it as a machine, as a Language Research Trainee, as a Prospective High-Prestige Academy Admission. He wrote it as a boy-turned-ape, going through the English Language Proficiency Motions. He wrote it as a dead thing, possessing a simulacrum of life. He wrote it under an internalized compulsion.

Let me explain. When you find someone doing something that is not recognizably human, that must have been dreary in the doing, and yet that pretends to express an enthusiasm that is not present and a thought that is stillborn, you should intuit a cause. If the whip is not applied to the flesh from without, it must be applied to the brain from within. The student above has been trained in cant. He feels he *must* reach for the Great Thought. That Thought *must* be "progressive," pretending to a delight in the fascinating world of up-to-the-minute fictional nonfiction and nonfictional fiction. It *must* take a certain number of Great Sentences to express, just as an absolute monarch progressing from the throne room to the royal tennis court must be preceded by lords in waiting, chamberlains, footmen, courtesans, and the holder of the royal tennis balls. The point is not that the paragraph is the result of a certain kind of training. It is that only training, and not true education, could produce such a paragraph.

The passage is unrelieved by the slightest touch of beauty or elegance, of human feeling, of real address to a world of trees and dandelions and dogs. There is one obvious observation—we have computers and the Internet. There is no wisdom, nor even the sprightly bravado of youth. The writing is senile without ever having been young.

Is that too harsh? Not when our foremen hold this essay forth as exemplary. We could hardly expect any better when the archons themselves write in a clodhopping pastiche of political lingo and social-science lingo, impossible to parody. Presumably they have been too busy processing "information" to have learned how to read, either.

But why should we care? Won't this bad idea die the death? I'm not so sanguine. Our bad ideas both induce compulsions and spring from compulsions. This particular bad idea is part of a federal measure called Race to the Top (RTTT, for bureaucrats playing with blocks). Here's a rare example of a directive whose name actually reveals something essential. Not, of course, what the directors think it reveals. The directors believe that all this stress upon linguistic "skills" will help us achieve the summit of the, the . . . we're not sure, but it will be the summit! What it really reveals is Life Under Compulsion.

What's the race? Why the induced panic? Is someone somewhere going to invent some new form of mass marketing and human degradation before we do? Say it ain't so! Is that little child going to waste his time *being*, rather than doing, and doing what his betters want him to do, and when, and why, and how? Is he going to read books for the joy of reading and for the human wisdom to be gleaned from them? Is he going to write meditations upon them without dutifully scrounging up professional sources, focusing on what makes for careers?

The demon Uncle Screwtape reproaches Wormwood for allowing his charge to take a walk in the country to an old mill. Can't have that, and can't read a book for the pleasure in reading it, rather than for the smoky antipleasure of saying pert things about it, picking out "sources" from the sludge of the Internet in the way that beggars pick out lice from the snarls of their hair, and making your way among people who matter. I'd say that Screwtape runs our whole educational machine, but that does an injustice to the avuncular one. He at least can write.

You Are Obsolete

Another scene, from Rod Serling's *Twilight Zone*. The series is often called science fiction, because sometimes there was travel to other planets. That's a misleading description. What it really featured were morality plays—Greek tragedies and Christian comedies, and sometimes a little of both at once. Both are at work here.

A stern, strong-jawed man in military uniform stands at his exalted table of judgment. He glares down at a little old man below. The old man has been haled before the court on the charge that he is "obsolete." He is of no *use*. His name, fittingly enough, is Romney Wordsworth, and he is a librarian. "A librarian," says the chancellor with infinite scorn. The state has no need of such!

It would have been easy for viewers in Serling's day to identify the chancellor as something like a Nazi or a Soviet puppet. At one point he thunders, "The state has proven that there is no God!"

"There is a God!" says the librarian. "You cannot erase God with an edict!"

What is at stake here is far more than censorship, far more than the evils of one or two mad nations in the twentieth century. It is a battle between incompatible views of human life. The view associated with a sterile, insane, and inhuman future combines the power of the state with the mechanistic assumptions of bad science. The view associated with the immemorial past—with the books that once stood in the library where Mr. Wordsworth worked, before the state destroyed it—is that the nature of man does not change, and that a man cannot be obsolete, because he is made in the image of God.

In this evil land, which in many ways is our land, what cannot be shown to serve an obvious utilitarian end is condemned as obsolete, and the punishment for obsolescence is death. We hear the condemnations all the time. Anyone who holds to a way of life more than three minutes old is a Neanderthal or worse. He must be swept into the trash. Mr. Wordsworth—Romney, William, Christopher—must be swept into the trash.

Mr. Romney Wordsworth, though, turns the tables on the chancellor. The chancellor has the slogans of science, the future, and the state. Wordsworth has the truths of the poets, the historians, and the philosophers. And more than those: he has long secreted away his most precious possession, the book most feared by our machinists of teaching—the Bible.

The state allows the condemned detritus of progress to choose his method of death. Wordsworth accordingly specifies that his execution must be televised; it will occur in his room; and he wants a representative of the state to be present. The chancellor himself shows up, gloating. But then Wordsworth reveals to him one additional detail. He has locked the door to his apartment. He wants the people watching on television to see the difference between how a man meets death and how a creature of the state meets it. For a bomb will go off at midnight precisely, killing both him and the chancellor. And let not the official think that he can plead with his fellow totalitarians to rescue him; no, that would show the state to be weak indeed.

The minutes pass. Wordsworth takes out his Bible and begins to read from the Psalms. "The Lord is my shepherd," he says. "I shall not want. He maketh me to lie down in green pastures; he leadeth me beside the still waters; he restoreth my soul." The chancellor paces, sweats, mutters, pleads.

"The fool hath said in his heart, There is no God," Wordsworth says.

It is almost the moment of death when the chancellor breaks down and cries, "Please! Please! In the name of God, let me out!"

"In the name of God, I will let you out," says the old man, and the chancellor escapes only a few seconds before the room explodes.

But when the chancellor returns to the place of judgment, his second-in-command, a man with the voice and demeanor of a robot, has assumed his place. "You are obsolete," he says to the chancellor. The jury surrounds the obsolete man, droning, threatening, like military machines moving in for a kill.

Behold an image of freedom. An old man sits in his apartment, reading words that have lifted the hearts and souls of millions of men before him, because the words point to a truth that calls us forth in adoration and that cannot be reduced to a scientific formula or a political program. He sits and he reads the twenty-third psalm. He can never be obsolete so long as there are still men in the world.

Behold an image of compulsion. The chancellor scorns the words of Scripture. He has no *use* for the poets. He falls down before the god of the state, with sophisticated technology at its beck. He is secretly a weakling, and that is why he *must* call upon instruments of mass compulsion. He looks to the future, because he can fill its emptiness with his mad dreams of power. He envies the man who drinks living water from the wellsprings of the past. He envies the man who can sit in his room quietly and pray to God.

Again I ask: What sort of child shall you raise, my readers?

3

Rush to Work

The Treadmill

M illions of women rose up, said G. K. Chesterton, to declare that they would no longer be dictated to, and promptly became stenographers.

Why do we work? What is work for? Why, with all our wealth, do we feel *compelled* to work, as if it measured the worth of our existence?

Here I turn to a fascinating conversation in *The Burning Bush*, by Sigrid Undset. Two grown cousins, Paul and Ruth, are speaking of their work and the upbringing their mothers received from their grandparents. Paul is a man with a minor talent for art and a great deal of talent for philosophical thought. But he works as a businessman, dealing in stone and other commodities during the First World War. He is drawing near to the Catholic faith; Undset herself entered the Catholic Church as an adult and something of an early feminist. Ruth is a painter in a minor way, whose works Paul sells. Ruth is unmarried. Paul is married to a lovely, shallow, and difficult woman and is more or less contented with his lot. They are speaking about work.

Ruth had some talent, and her father, whom she describes as "terribly naive and emancipated and all that," took it into his head that she had to go to art school. Note the irony. The father is "emancipated," meaning that he has knocked the manacles from his mind, and that means that his daughter Ruth *must* damned well be emancipated too, emancipated right into school, work, and a life alone. Ruth is not bitter about it, but she sees that there might have been something far better for her as a human being, and even a better use for her artistic talent:

> Actually, you know, grandmother Randall for instance got a great deal more out of her accomplishments, when she made drawings of the houses they lived in and did water-colors of grandfather and their children or of baskets of flowers. She could afford to be an amateur—literally an amateur of all that she thought pretty, for she played and sang too, and wrote the most enchanting letters. Not to mention their financial difficulties and that grandfather was not an easy man to live with and she had his parents in the house and had seven children and lost five of them while they were young. But she had the chance of using all her powers in the order which seemed natural to her, so no doubt she always felt free. So that both your mother and mine were able to grow up to maturity with sunshine all about them.

The grandmother could "afford" to be an amateur, literally a *lover of things*. Ruth is careful to note that it was not money that made her able to afford it. The finances were always strapped; they had a lot of children, and a couple of elderly parents to care for. The affordability, the "chance," was not monetary but cultural. The grandmother was not compelled to specialize, as Chesterton had noted. She could go in for everything whose beauty she loved: painting, playing the piano, singing, letter writing, and all the rest of the daily arts that make for a home. These things shed as warm an influence upon the children she raised as the sun sheds upon the world.

Paul understands her and tries to offer a modest defense of the emancipated woman. The grandfather "was a domestic tyrant," and there are plenty of men who are only too glad "if they could get off having to provide for their unmarried daughters and sisters":

So they haven't worried about who is to perform the work of culture properly so called which we men are incapable of taking a hand in. I have often thought of that, when I look at my own lady clerks and others like them—they certainly possess treasures of humanity sufficient to have charge of a whole flock of children and to be allowed to form them during the years which are of most importance. And there are thousands and thousands of men who might be put in a subordinate position without any loss to the world.

This "work of culture" springs from the haven of the home, and no number of titanic sculptures in a public square can make up for it. Paul blames the men for the loss, because they allow women who are *indispensable as culture makers* in the home to become *dispensable and interchangeable* in the workplace, and indeed *subordinate*, while many a man instead might drudge his days away as a clerk and not be missed.

Ruth laughs and pokes gentle fun at Paul's feminist mother: "Aunt Julie would call that taking part in the work of culture—the great work of culture which consists in putting as many people as possible into situations subject to short notice, or making them irremovable State functionaries." In other words, you are *free* if you must show up at a certain place at a certain time, to do a certain well-defined and usually narrow thing, for a certain salary, or else be fired. You are *not free* if you are Ruth's grandmother in the home, ordering her days as she sees fit, sometimes washing and cooking, sometimes painting, making clothing for her children, teaching them songs, telling them stories while weaving, and doing those things out of love. You are *free* if you push papers for a boss for nine hours a day or scrape the plaque from the teeth of strangers with bad breath. You are *not free* if you take the time to write enchanting letters. You are *free* if you deliver other people's letters in a mailbag.

Sigrid Undset wrote these words in 1930, long before Josef Pieper's *Leisure: The Basis of Culture*. Pieper notes that the word that gives us our name for the place where children are taught, the Latin *schola*, properly means not school but leisure. It is where you learn the arts proper to a free man: the liberal arts. We have adopted, he suggests, tracing the error to Immanuel Kant, a kind of Prussian attitude toward what is good and praiseworthy. Kant said that an action merits praise only insofar as it runs athwart one's natural inclinations. What you don't have to sweat and strain for means nothing. The more sensible and human way to look at virtue, though, is the one adopted by Aristotle and Thomas Aquinas: it is a habit, a "second nature," that allows you to do what is good *without effort*. As a healthy man need not be conscious of his legs as he strides or runs, so the man of virtue does what is right by moral health and strength. The habit sets him free to achieve the perfecting of his human nature. He is temperate without a regimen, courageous without a captain, wise without an overseer, just without the threat of juries.

But we now live, says Pieper, in a culture of "total work." That does not mean that all people are always laboring. It means that whatever they are doing, even if they are unemployed, even if they leech from their neighbors, they see no real value in anything that is not work. In our time, either they are hamsters treading the mills that light the lights or they gaze at the screens lit by their fellow hamsters. Their sin, both ways, is sloth—the inability to delight in what should properly bring us joy. Or, to put it in terms of Life Under Compulsion, they can be lazy, but they can never be at ease. They must be up and doing, or down and consuming.

No Barefoot Boys

Our contemporary educators believe it is their duty to introduce young students to other "cultures," by which is meant writers and artists of certain preferred ethnic groups, who watch the same television we watch, listen to the same canned music on the radio, read the same aphatic magazines, attend the same institutional schools, and frequent the same slick-slop restaurants. But if educators really wished to introduce students to a wholly foreign way of life, they might direct their attention to something other than the treadmill. For that, all they'd need is to dust off a few of their own old schoolbooks.

I have, before me, the *Eighth Year* of the Literature Readers series for California schools, published in 1917. An old note has clung to the inside of the back cover. Its heading is Alhambra City Schools, Alhambra, California. The note, in gentle feminine cursive, reads:

Dear Mrs. Montgomery:
   You are cordially invited to attend an exhibit given by the 8a
   class of 1926 June 18, from 10:30 to 12:00, Room 8 of the Ynez
   School.

One dearly wishes to know what that exhibit was about. If it held to the spirit of the eighth reader, it wouldn't have had much to do with careerism. The editor of the book, Leroy Armstrong, did not believe in the Life Under Compulsion, into which children must be ushered, so that their reading assignments would prepare them to be flywheels in a global economy. Quite the contrary.

Armstrong has two goals in mind, which he expresses with admirable brevity in an introductory "Talk with the Teacher." First, he wishes students to acquire "the library habit." He hopes his reader will introduce students to good books so that they will want to read more—books of literary merit, not those that corrupt or evacuate the mind. He says his reader will have succeeded if it results in a classroom wherein thirty pupils are quietly reading thirty different books, with the teacher as their kindly overseer.

What will be the point of such reading? Nothing utilitarian. Armstrong is one of those wise schoolmen who know the limitations of schooling. This leads him to his second goal. We may first find literature in school, but its poetry has for its end neither school nor work but something forgotten by people who live under compulsion:

With the library habit as the goal, there will be a clearer understanding of the real function of literature. Nearly all the school
subjects lay great stress on information. But literature makes its
appeal to the heart as well as the intellect. Geography and arith-
metic fit a pupil for hours of labor in later life. *Literature pre-
pares him for the hours of leisure now and later* [emphasis mine].
Literature makes the pupil a good companion for himself, and
removes the appeal of cheap entertainments and unworthy
companions. Literature is essentially non-informational, and
finds its glory and its charm in that fact. No Gradgrind, bent
on facts, should ever be persuaded to teach a class in literature.

It's impossible for me to imagine that any editor of a textbook
could write those words today. The words are too clear, too sane, too
healthy. Notice that Armstrong drops the name Gradgrind, assuming
that the teacher will have read Dickens's *Hard Times* and will understand what is wrong with that schoolmaster's poetry-despising utili-
tarianism. Notice, too, that he elevates leisure above labor. The sense
is not that literature is for "spare time," minutes snatched from the
relentless clock. Nor is it for consumption, gobbling up what allays
the hedonist within. It's rather that, in leisure, the grown man can
enjoy that freedom which is the true end of labor. It is a spiritual freedom, as of someone walking along a mill path for the sheer peaceful
beauty; without it, as Pieper warns us—and Undset has anticipated
him in the insight—we have no culture at all. In that leisure, he can
pick up a good old book as if he were to call upon an old friend, and
converse with the author, and the world, and the ages.

It's no surprise, then, that the literature Armstrong selects should
often reflect this spiritual freedom. One of the lighter pieces is John
Greenleaf Whittier's poem "The Barefoot Boy." Whittier begins by
wishing blessings upon that boy, bare of foot and tan of face, his pants
legs turned up, his straw hat torn at the brim, and a whistled tune on
his lips. He blesses him because he was once that boy, and there is
hardly a finer thing on earth to be:

Prince thou art—the grown-up man
Only is republican.
Let the million-dollared ride!
Barefoot, trudging at his side,
Thou hast more than he can buy
In the reach of ear and eye—
Outward sunshine, inward joy:
Blessings on thee, barefoot boy!

The boy is a prince; the man is but a republican. Armstrong will ask, in his deft questions that follow the poem, what Whittier may have meant by that. It bears some contemplation. Whittier explains it in part by the contrast between the millionaire in his conveyance and the boy, walking. The millionaire has his money and his expensive toys. The boy has the world.

What world? The sweet, exuberant, manifold, dangerous, fascinating world wherein he learns

Knowledge never learned of schools,
Of the wild bee's morning chase,
Of the wild-flower's time and place,
Flight of fowl and habitude
Of the tenants of the wood;
How the tortoise bears his shell,
How the woodchuck digs his cell,
And the ground-mole sinks his well;
How the robin feeds her young,
How the oriole's nest is hung;
Where the whitest lilies blow,
Where the freshest berries grow,
Where the ground-nut trails its vine,
Where the wood-grape's clusters shine;
Of the black wasp's cunning way,
Mason of his walls of clay,

And the architectural plans
Of gray hornet artisans!
For, eschewing books and tasks,
Nature answers all he asks;
Hand in hand with her he walks,
Face to face with her he talks,
Part and parcel of her joy,—
Blessings on the barefoot boy!

Are these things no longer here to behold? Or is there no time
to behold them? Surely that boy had plenty of chores to do at home.
Whittier is recalling his own boyhood, growing up on a farm, and
that meant work. What, then, devours our time? What has built
walls, ten feet thick and padded within, between us and that world?

I live in New England, and I know that everything Whittier
describes is still here. The orioles arrive in April, their loud clear
songs making a hundred yards seem a few feet away. They still build
their pendulous nests in the treetops, but nobody knows it. There are
still wild grapevines everywhere, and at times in September you can
breathe that rich half-drunken mustiness and know that high above
in the treetops there's fruit, gallons of purple grapes, that only the
birds and squirrels can reach. That world is still here, like a forgotten
stranger. The natural light of the sun still shines, but men do not love
the light.

These days we have no true childhood, only a diseased precocity,
introducing children to things that any decent man of Whittier's day,
or of Armstrong's, would have considered unutterably vile. Therefore we have no true adulthood either, only a prolonged infantility, a
curdled adolescence followed by old age and death. Just as we cannot
have culture without leisure as its foundation, the leisure of contemplation and worship, so we cannot have a fruitful adulthood without that barefoot boy dwelling within. This has nothing to do with
laziness. It has to do with a healthy and reverent orientation of one's
whole being. It is deeply religious.

Whittier turns serious as he brings his poem to a close. For boy-hood cannot last forever. He wishes, for this boy, not "success" in the world but something infinitely more to be treasured:

All too soon these feet must hide
In the prison cells of pride,
Lose the freedom of the sod,
Like a colt's for work be shod,
Made to tread the mills of toil,
Up and down in ceaseless moil;
Happy if their track be found
Never on forbidden ground;
Happy if they sink not in
Quick and treacherous sands of sin.
Ah! that thou couldst know thy joy,
Ere it passes, barefoot boy!

The feet will be shod, for work, or worse—for pride, for sin. But if that boy could know his happiness before it passes and understand what makes so blessed his innocent life among the lowly creatures, then he would know also how to avoid the quicksand, to survive the grinding of the machine. He would know, in part, the glorious liberty of the children of God.

Play and No Play

What if we have a whole town full of people who in some measure have experienced that liberty? What might it look like?

In East Bangor, Pennsylvania (population 800), there's a little diner named for the trolley that used to take people to the once-bustling steel town of Bethlehem. The proprietors have adorned the walls with photographs of other local things that are no more. There's one of the East Bangor band, a group of about twenty men and boys, in uniform, in front of a bandstand draped with bunting. There's also one of the Kaysers, a local baseball club, on the day of an exhibition ballgame against the Philadelphia Athletics. These were Connie Mack's A's, which team in those early 1930s featured Hall of Famers Jimmie Foxx, Mickey Cochrane, and Lefty Grove.

How did a village of under a thousand people manage to have its own band? How did a cluster of slate-belt villages field a regular baseball club, apparently good enough to stay on the same field for nine innings with the Philadelphia Athletics?

What happened to music and the arts has also happened to sport, and the schools, those engines of compulsion, have been at the center of the transformation. Until fairly recently, most people's experience of sport was direct and personal. Take baseball. You played it, or you watched others play it a few feet in front of you as you sat in the bleachers with your neighbors. Every little town had a ball club. Some of these were what we'd call the minor leagues, which were independent leagues and not just the serfs of the major leagues; they had their own races, their own lifelong stars, and their own loyal fans. Other clubs were semiprofessional, a way for a man to pick up a few extra dollars. But there were many thousands of them. Christy Mathewson, a Pennsylvania boy, broke in as a pitcher for a team in Honesdale, a little village in the boondocks. Stan Coveleski, same state, broke in as a pitcher for a team in the coal town of Shamokin. Teams even came from big factories and mills.

Those clubs were the public and organized manifestation of what was going on everywhere, with informal self-organization or without any organization at all. Boys would make their own teams and play other self-made teams, long before the Little League. Schools got in on the action, too—and here is where the story grows strange.

As in so many other bad things, the Ivy League schools took the lead. In the late 1800s they became the first to grant scholarships to young men for athletic prowess, so that the Princeton footballers under President McCosh could leave their Yale rivals in the mud. It was innocent enough, a desire to unite the small community of scholars around something boisterous and manly, with the bruisers stiff-arming the Eli tacklers while the slenderer men with the megaphones cried out, "Tiger tiger tiger sis sis sis boom boom boom bah!" But it did not remain small and innocent. Nor did it remain free. It has been conscripted into Life Under Compulsion.

When high schools were small and local, they might field a couple of sports teams, usually the big three, baseball, football, and basketball, with hockey thrown in for the ice belt. There were a lot more of those teams than there are now, proportional to the school population, because there were a lot more schools. There was also no way to take any one school's success too seriously. No national ranking of high school teams was conceivable. Boys could play on a team whose school had a senior class of thirty or forty, as my mother's did, in Archbald, Pennsylvania; many of those boys could never make the squad for a school ten times as large. As for other sports, like golf or tennis or swimming, you played them because you enjoyed the competition, not because the school had a team for it.

Consolidation changed all of that, and was in part sold by the prospect of a wider array of sports. One small school could not afford a "natatorium"—the cement pond—but one enormous school could pretend to. Those programs, in turn, fed college sports, so that parents of an athletic child (and soon girls would be shunted into the grinder) could parlay his skill in hitting a ball or running fast into that plum, the inaptly named "scholarship." This scholarship is sold, too, as a prize, or a gift, rather than partial forgiveness of a debt that exceeds the human value of what professors teach or students learn.

But Johnny Friendly the Boss is handing out favors, so everyone must compete to win one, or be squeezed to death. I have nothing against athletic competition, that boyish and dynamic form of cooperation that lay at the foundation of the Greek polis. I am noting two things. The first is that, after all these programs and scholarships, after all the work done by organized athletics at all levels, the number of boys actually playing baseball or football is far lower than before: no one is outdoors playing. The second is implied by the first. If they're not outdoors playing, where are they? If they're not athletes, they are indoors, alone, wasting time, distracting themselves from their distraction. There are no Kaysers, no teams in Shamokin or Honesdale, and, for that matter, no village band. If they are athletes, they are working. That's what we have done. We have eliminated most play and turned the rest into work.

Why? When I see young people caught in the athletic-scholastic mill, I seldom sense that they delight in it. They are committed to it. They may enjoy the games or the meets. But the whole thing, the many hours of running, lifting, practice, all to seize that scholarship apple or to keep from having it snatched away—what is it for? Does it lift the spirit? Does it set them free?

Behind them stand the parents, or the school, suggesting, "You have a talent in gymnastics. You want to succeed at this, don't you? It will help you get into that private high school. Even if you aren't recruited for a college team, it will look good on your dossier. It will help you get into college. It will give you a wider range of colleges from which to choose. If you are recruited, it means scholarship money. Look at what happened to Kelly. She had her picture in the newspaper when she won the gold medal at the state meet. You're just as good as she is, or you can be if you try hard enough." And so forth.

We can trace out a nice chain of compulsions, thus. Mr. and Mrs. Ergonome are moving to a new state. They choose to live in a "good" neighborhood—set apart from the unwashed—for the sake of a "good" school, a well-funded factory that produces "college material," the half-finished industrial stuff that is then transformed into transistors, gas engines, and Styrofoam packing. To secure this good school, they buy a house beyond their means. To pay the mortgage, Mrs. Ergonome must earn a salary outside the home. To enable Mrs. Ergonome to do that, they must purchase a second car, and day care for the two children. They choose the "best" day care, the one brightest in Plasticine, and with relatively few of the unwashed (although

Mr. and Mrs. Ergonome, upholding the dignity of people they flee, would deny any such motive). That, too, is a noose for the budget.

Mr. and Mrs. Ergonome want their two children to go to college, because, what with the schools as bad as they are (but, presto! it's other people's schools, never ours), employers have resorted to requiring a college degree. They do this not for anything the employee may have learned in college but to ensure that he will be able to read and count, and will show up on time. It's a mechanism, that's all. It helps keep the government overseer off their backs, lest they exert a human judgment not approved by their betters. So the kids have to go to college, and it has to be a good college, its worth determined by utility. Therefore the kids have to be groomed and trimmed for it right now. And sport, dance, gymnastics, scouting, community "service," every blessed thing that can go on a résumé will go on the résumés of the Ergonome offspring. Human life is for sale.

Noise

This worship of work for work's sake, this climbing upon the treadmill because the treadmill is reliable and pays well and requires nothing of our souls, is a kind of noisy diversion from the human condition. Pascal, in his *Pensées*, wrote that if you simply gave a man the money he wanted to win at the gaming table, he would be disappointed, because the last thing he really wants is the silence. "I have discovered that all the unhappiness of men arises from one single fact, that they cannot stay quietly in their own chamber." He does not mean that we should not walk outdoors or that we should not work. He means instead that we use the commotion of work, the chase, licentiousness, and warfare to keep ourselves distracted. The Benedictine monks, whose motto is *"Ora et labora"*—"Work and pray"—founded themselves upon the stability of place and the richness of silence. Our motto instead is, "Work—or do anything at all, so long as you do not pray, or even come to an awareness of your frailty." Turn up the noise.

Most people now do not have to endure the ear-battering din of the great factories of the Industrial Revolution. But what was deafening then in decibels was not yet distracting in triviality. A thunderstorm is loud, but if it is outside of our walls, it can be strangely peaceful, too. It can be an opportunity for self-collection. The noise I am talking about here is different. It is essentially distracting, and it is both the environment in which we work and the very object of our work. It is almost as if we do not believe we are really at work unless there are noises, by which I mean all things that prevent not only interesting conversation but also human thought.

"What is the proper object of sight?" said the professor at Thomas Aquinas College, where I was visiting. He sat back then and waited. The students thought. Someone began to speak, venturing an answer. The students thought about it some more, and another one offered an amendment. So it went for more than an hour. Sometimes the conversation was sharp and quick. Sometimes it was leisurely, and you could hear the woodpeckers from the window. The professor allowed the conversation to continue, with only the lightest guidance.

I wasn't aware of it then, but the professor and his intelligent and philosophical students were more *childlike*, in the best sense of that word, than anyone I had ever seen in the midst of hard work. I will let the philosopher Max Picard explain. In *The World of Silence* (1952), Picard writes:

> The child's language is melodious. The words hide and protect themselves in the melody—the words that have come shyly out of the silence. They almost disappear again in the silence. There is more melody than content in the words of the child.
>
> It is as though silence were accumulating within the child as a reserve for the adult, for the noisy world of the child's later years as an adult. The adult who has preserved within himself not only something of the language of childhood but also something of its silence, too, has the power to make others happy.

I know a boy—he is a young man now—whose parents took him to spend the summer every year with their kinfolk in the Spanish countryside. That was, outside of the village, a place of vast silences, the dry plains, the sun, the hard shadows of rocks, the scrub olives, the lizards and the birds and the flies. He would leave home in the morning with a small lunch and journey out into that silence, not returning until suppertime. Then he would take out his saxophone and play, and the girls from the village would gather round, and it was as if the great gift of the rocks and hills, their mysterious *being*, had found a voice in that horn. He did not so much break the silence as give it form and extend it to others.

In silence, the young Wordsworth rowed out onto the big lake and saw the mountain looming up against him, a vast intimation of a presence in the world that is beyond human naming. In silence, Michelangelo lay upon the scaffolding in the Sistine Chapel, sheltered from the noisy streets below, and painted the unpaintable silence of Adam, the moment before he received from God the breath of life and became a living soul.

When Cordelia hears the noisy protestations of her sisters, she turns to the secret springs of life within her: "What shall Cordelia speak? Love, and be silent." She will not, even at the prompting of her foolish father, King Lear, try to speak what cannot be spoken. Such were the words of lovers in times where true childhood had time to flourish. They were like gentle attempts to touch a hand to a hand. They were reticent before the mystery.

"Proper education and proper teaching," writes Max Picard, "are based on the substance of silence." For silence, he asserts, is not an absence but a presence. It is noise, rather, that is the absence, both of the significant word and of the fullness of being that silence allows us to hear. Silence belongs to man as the creature who possesses the word; noise, to the creature whom words possess, lashing him on, on, mechanically, without rest, without meaning.

Stimulus: The Instrument of Utility

The boy has taken up the book and turns to Isaiah. He sees numbers and small headings. Each word on the page is like a living creature. He can read the words, but he cannot yet reduce them to insignificance. He cannot trap them and kill them, stuff them with his own knowledge and put them on a shelf. He wants to watch the living creature. He wants to follow it, as if you could tiptoe into its cave and enter another world.

He is not being "stimulated." We who do not have the word have forgotten how petty and dreary a thing it is to be stimulated. The *stimulus* is the prick or spur you dig into the side of an animal. Imagine the horse, slow-moving creature when he is content, with his large, sad eyes. If we are to make use of him, we must apply the spur. The stimulus is the instrument of utility. In a world where even human beings are no more than occasions for profit, the stimulus is everywhere. It is as if everyone were wearing a hair shirt, not to mortify the flesh but to nag it, to keep it from resting, to *stimulate* it.

Everything is a stinging nettle. We drive down the street and the signs nettle us: buy this, do that. We enter a public place and the music that is not music nettles us. We look at the spines of books and their large letters in unnatural colors nettle us. Libraries are prickle beds of visual noise. Textbooks for children are so much noise; then the restlessness of the classroom; the political sloganeering; the inevitable exam; the "enlightened" urging of the parents; the sting, the lash of prestige, of seeking admittance to the "best" school, the "best" team, the "best" club; the noise of a clanking death-in-life. Then to escape one noise, the children turn to another, the prick of the video game, the tweet, the drug, the sexual hook.

It is essentially a pornographic world, where everyone lies naked on a bed of nettles, and every new thing is dead before it is born. Do we doubt this? Consider an advertisement on television for a brand of beer, a ball game, a political party, or deodorant. Take from it everything that smacks of enticement to lust, wrath, avarice, envy, vanity, and pride. Take all the noise out of the noise. Take the sting from the nettles. There is nothing left.

Silence is so great a blessing to us because we cannot *use* it. All things truly creative, which partake of the spirit of play, send their roots deep down into silence. Watch the play of children when they are given time to play, and an outdoors for play, without the direction—the stimuli—of goading and noisome parents. People say that children at play are noisy. That is not true. They may whoop and holler and laugh, they may be heard from far off, but they aren't making *noise*. When an old man hears the cries of boys playing ball in a field around the corner, it is as if time had returned to its home in eternity, and the field of his youth had never gone away.

When Jesus said, "Suffer little children, and forbid them not, to come unto me: for of such is the kingdom of heaven," perhaps He meant to recommend more than humility and innocence. For the great power of childhood is its direct address to the mystery of being. The child is not yet swept up into the world of profit and loss. He plays, and it is like contemplation. He prays, and it is like play. Even the dialogues of Plato, says Picard, partake of a kind of childhood, because when the play of conversation is over, the characters seem to let the silence settle among them again, as we can imagine Socrates and Phaedrus resting a little while longer under the plane tree on the road from Athens.

What do we now mean by "education" if not efficiently directed stimuli, profitable noise? We teach young people to encounter great works of art as if they were noise, prating about themselves and, Lord forgive us, about their creators, nagging us to prate about them in our turn. And in all of this senile prattle what is lost but the beautiful work itself, and the child, and the speaking silence between them?

We cannot educate young people, because we no longer understand what people are for. We are the creatures who behold, who play, who give a tongue to silence. That is one of the things meant by the verse "Let us make man in our image."

4

Forgetting How to Think

The Idiot

"I don't teach my students *what* to think," I have heard teachers say a thousand times, with an air of pride. "I teach my students *how* to think."

Reach for your wallet when you hear it. There is no such thing as human thought, free-floating, unattached from things to think about, things that possess their own integrity and that must in large part determine how we are to think about them. That is another way of saying that there is no such thing as human language, unattached from things to speak about and from their ways of being. To say that you know how to think but do not much care for the truth is to reduce thought to a series of vague impressions, none of them really worth remembering. You might as well say that you know how to use a hammer but do not care for wood and nails, or for tables, chairs, porches, stairs, and walls.

It is, finally, a denial of the fundamental reality affirmed in different words by the beloved disciple and the Greek philosophers: *In the beginning was the Word.*

Let us examine now the disintegration of social and political language, and its relation to Life Under Compulsion.

A Stupid Soul

Our first occupant of the idiot house comes from Dante's *Inferno*. The poets are in a strange border area between the frauds and the traitors, abusers of language both. In this area we find the Giants, mainly the Titans from Greek mythology, who attempted to shoulder Zeus from his throne not by being great but by being *big*—in other words, by sheer dumb brute force.

Suddenly they hear a blast from a horn so loud it seems to shake the realm of Hell, like the trumpet call that resounded in Roncesvalles when the brave Roland in the rear guard of Charlemagne's army was ambushed by Saracens and called for assistance from the king. Remember that trumpet and its signifying note. It meant, "I need your help!" It meant, "I have been betrayed by one of our own number!" It meant, as Charlemagne saw when he finally arrived amid the thousands of Christian dead, "I am giving my life for you, my liege lord!"

Then they see where the blast has come from. A giant figure, fixed in a kind of well, stands staring at them with fury. He has a horn strapped around him. Then he "speaks," spewing gibberish:

> "Raphèl maí amècche zabí almi,"
> the savage mouth began to shout at us;
> no sweeter psalm was fit for such as he.
> And my guide turned against him: "Stupid soul!
> Grab your horn tight and vent yourself with it
> when wrath or any passion seizes you!"

Dante has done something fascinating here. He has taken the story of the Tower of Babel and located its meaning in a certain kind of pride. For the builders of Babel wanted a tower to reach unto the heavens, lest they come under the domination of their neighbors. They wanted "to make a name for themselves," to cow other men into submission.

The punishment is a dissolution of language, here seen as the one means by which human beings unite. The builders can no longer understand one another, and so their tower remains no more than a ruin. To a poet like Dante, who had meditated all his life on the power and the meaning of language, the story is filled with admonitory lessons.

Think of that tower. One way to consider its evil and its folly is to think of it as man's attempt, *on his own*, to sit in the heavens with God—not to wait upon God's revelation, not to hear the word of God, but to ignore that gift and to drown out the divine word with a merely human word, actually a merely utilitarian word. The tower says, "This is the ladder by which we will ascend the heavens." Another way to consider its evil and its folly is to think of it as man's attempt to advertise himself as a being of divine might, against God and against *other men*. It is as if to say, "You *must* speak about me! I am powerful, my head strikes the heavens!" So the tower is at once an act of deceit, of the self-flattery that stultifies those who engage in it, and of treason. A far cry from the call of the loyal Roland, driven to it by the last extremity of danger and self-sacrifice.

Notice, too, that the horn around Nimrod's neck is but a mechanical device for use when he *must* vent his wrath. He is reduced to a kind of animate *thing*, with no more choice in the matter than he has capacity to express himself. The gibberish means nothing to him and nothing to anyone else. Ironically enough, his first word in the mangled Hebrew suggests the name Raphael, the angel who helped the boy Tobias regain his father's eyesight when the Jews lived in captivity: it means *God heals*.

Percy Shelley picked up the cue from Dante and applied it to foolish tyrants everywhere:

I met a traveller from an antique land
Who said—"Two vast and trunkless legs of stone
Stand in the desert. Near them, on the sand,
Half sunk, a shattered visage lies, whose frown,

And wrinkled lip, and sneer of cold command,
Tell that its sculptor well those passions read
Which yet survive, stamped on these lifeless things,
The hand that mocked them and the heart that fed.
And on the pedestal these words appear:
'My name is Ozymandias, King of Kings:
Look on my Works, ye Mighty, and despair!'
Nothing beside remains. Round the decay
Of that colossal Wreck, boundless and bare
The lone and level sands stretch far away."

Notice the terrible contrast between what the statue says—the wrinkled lip, the sneer, the mocking hand, the vain boast engraved upon the pedestal—and what the statue means. It is a great nothing. It stands in the midst of nothingness, the vast unmeaning desert, the sands where no man lives, level to the horizon, miles upon endless miles. Its words are like the splurting nonsense of Nimrod, like the note of the giant's trumpet, calling out an alarm for nothing, to no one, and so on forever.

"But we are in no danger of falling prey to such foolish tyrants," I hear the objection from the crowd. "We believe in democracy." Alexis de Tocqueville, who wrote about the United States when it was still a fledgling, noted that democracy can make common cause with tyranny quite well, for along with a "manly and lawful passion for equality . . . there exists also in the human heart a depraved taste for equality, which impels the weak to attempt to lower the powerful to their own level and reduces men to prefer equality in slavery to inequality with freedom." It is not only princes who lap up flattery, while their ministers and valets play them like puppets. The masses lap it up, too.

It is precisely because we believe in democracy as a talisman, a heal-all, that we are prone to the disintegration of language that characterizes Life Under Compulsion. It is true that our leaders, unlike Ozymandias, King of Kings, do not curl their lips and sneer at us from their pedestals. They do worse. They flatter us. They tell us they are 'umbled, quite 'umbled, that we should be so wise as to have chosen them. They tell us that our freedom consists not in what we choose but in the fact *that we choose*. They hold forth visions of our greatness to compass their own ends. Whether they believe the flattery may matter for the destination of their eternal souls, but it hardly alters the condition we live in.

We must be on constant guard against believing that democracy is a mechanical and automatic result of a certain governmental structure or certain electoral and legislative processes. Men are not machines; nor can they be governed by machines. To see that this is so, consider the question of numbers. The size of a legislative body: what is the best number of representatives? That question cannot be answered by theory, only by human experience. Five thousand is not necessarily better than five hundred, and it may be far worse. So James Madison suggests, in *The Federalist* 55:

> In all cases a certain number at least seems to be necessary to secure the benefits of free consultation and discussion, and to guard against too easy a combination for improper purposes; as, on the other hand, the number ought at most to be kept within a certain limit, in order to avoid the confusion and intemperance of a multitude. In all very numerous assemblies, of whatever character composed, passion never fails to wrest the sceptre from reason. Had every Athenian citizen been a Socrates, every Athenian assembly would still have been a mob.

Man governs himself by reason. Mobs hurl themselves into action and strife. They sow something more dangerous than dissension. They sow compulsions—like drugs of single-minded madness, injected into the soul.

The Founders knew that demagogues had embroiled democratic Athens in her disastrous war against Sparta. They knew that demagogues, or rather *the people of Athens themselves*, acting as a judicial mob, had put Socrates to death. They had heard the keen observation of Christ, who said that the heathen suffer their kings to lord it over them as their "benefactors," but "among you," He said, "it must not be so."

At its best, the electoral process is a handy tool for securing justice and the common good. But in Life Under Compulsion, that tool has become an idol. As long as you have it, you are free, and no one deprived of the tool can be free. You are free as long as you can choose—between a manacle and a fetter, a straitjacket or a cell, an exercise bicycle or a treadmill.

The women who led the resistance *against* suffrage argued that their opinions on social matters gained them greater respect precisely because they *did not* vote. They were not up for purchase by the highest political bidder. I'm not saying that their position was correct. I note only that it has become incomprehensible to us, which says more about us than it does about them. Sigrid Undset, to my mind the greatest woman novelist who ever lived, makes the plausible point that once women were entering the mercantile world alongside their brothers, it was only fair that they should be granted the privilege to vote for the lawmakers who might try to ruin their businesses. But she also notes that the principle that animates the mother—who creates things of beauty and use for the people she loves, in the home and its surroundings, not for pay but in the free generosity of her heart—is absolutely necessary if human life is to be worth living at all. Undset's wisdom, too, has become nearly incomprehensible to us. If you can vote, you are free, and if you cannot vote, you are not.

A truly free people needn't care overmuch about who is sitting on the throne or who has been elected representative to Parliament from Pocket Borough. They do not feel the compulsion to catch every flitting word of the day. They do more than live from empty speech to empty speech. They dwell in the long wisdom of the ages, the slowly won customs of their ancestors. They have, as it were, a clean well-lighted room in which to sit, to talk to their friends and their family, and to watch the sun setting upon the hills. Their property is safe from the depredation of thieves, lawyers, and foreign armies. Their children are safe from corruption and conscription. They live with their neighbors. This is the true democracy, and, as I have said, no mechanism for voting can guarantee it.

The Work of Stupefaction

Let us turn to George Orwell and his novel *Nineteen Eighty-Four*. Winston Smith, the alterer of history working at the Ministry of Truth, is at the lunch table with one of his colleagues, Syme. This fellow is a linguist with a passionate love for Newspeak, the official language of the regime. The purpose of Newspeak is to deracinate language so badly that *crimethought*, the *doubleplusungood* rebellion of mind against the regime, will be impossible. No one will be able to think of crimes, because nobody will be able to think, because they will lack language itself, the organ of thought. Syme is fascinated by the "beauty" of the destruction, which he describes with the passion of an intellectual. Smith says to himself that Syme knows too much, and in fact the day arrives when Syme is no longer to be seen.

Orwell's novels are required reading in many a school district in the English-speaking world. That is one of the immense ironies of our time. *De te fabula narratur!* Consider what Winston Smith does for a living. He does what our schools do. He rewrites history to fit the regime's propaganda. He erases evidence that things were ever otherwise than as the regime describes them. The job requires cleverness but also a demonic disintegration of the soul. You must violate the principle of noncontradiction. You must think yourself into believing what you know is false.

You must think yourself into believing that there is a developing child in Sally's womb, because Sally wants it, but only a parasitic blob in Sandy's womb, because Sandy does not. Indeed, you must believe that it can alter its being at the whim of the mother, from child to blob or from blob to child, depending upon her state of mind at the moment. You must believe that what is obviously human is not human, and what is obviously alive is not alive. You must call things by improper names: birth control instead of birth prevention, clinic instead of abattoir. The blaring propaganda of the radio and the television screen assists you in this slow intellectual suicide.

So do slogans, tics of the tongue. If you enter a school today, you are not likely to see the Ten Commandments, or other passages from Scripture, or from Homer or Shakespeare, gracing the walls of a classroom. You are likely to see large blaring self-celebratory pseudo-humanitarian slogans, proclaiming, "Dare to Be Unique," meaning, "Fall prey to the latest fad of self-absorption and self-advertisement!" If you observe the habits of men and women and note that other people observed them, too, three thousand years ago in Mesopotamia, two thousand years ago in Greece, a thousand years ago in medieval Italy, and across the seas in Japan and China, and you express what you have seen, as Homer did when the brave and blushing Nausicaa, a princess in the gleaming of first love, falls for Odysseus, so much manlier and more dangerous than the boys she's known all her life—if you do this, you will meet the scornful objection that has become automatic, that is, the predictable reaction of an automaton. "That's only a stereotype!" says the teacher, the politician, the sophomore, the television producer. Thought and love for truth are smothered in the cradle. If it moves, kill it.

You are also likely, at school, to find teachers who encourage their students in one of the basest of practices rewarded in Orwell's Oceania. That is, to rat on their parents. Teachers pass out questionnaires probing into what goes on in the home. Children are given the opportunity to retaliate against parents who, they believe, discipline them too harshly, even when the parents have committed nothing close to a crime. The social worker, under the rights-dissolving pretense of protecting the child, blows the front door off the home that used to be a castle and now is, in terms of its authority, a mud and wattle hut in the shadow of the state's impenetrable, labyrinthine fortress. Teachers are praised for instructing young people to *reject* the supposed prejudices of their parents, and their supposed ignorance.

When Ham revealed the nakedness of his old and drunken father, Noah, his brothers, Shem and Japheth, placed a blanket over the old man, walking backward so that they could not see the embarrassing sight. We raise a generation of young people like Ham.

In Orwell's novel, Winston Smith is witness to this enmity against the parent when he is tossed into prison for *thoughtcrime* and meets there his neighbor Parsons. This Parsons is a big bluff fellow, all for the regime, patriotic and compliant, but apparently, unconsciously, he has been seething against the benefactions of Big Brother. And one time when he was dozing his children overheard him muttering, "Down with Big Brother!" And duly turned him in to the police. Parsons is terrified by what he fears will happen to him now, but he is proud of his children, or says he is proud of them.

So it is that children, whose minds should be ranging the mountains of India with Kipling's Kim, or floating down the Mississippi with Huck and Jim, or saddling their horses in the Iberian plains beside the Knight of the Mournful Countenance, are "liberated" into a false, cramped, shallow world of slogans. They act out what the debased language expresses. Consider those chilling commercials, apparently now the preferred way of preaching to obstinate and insufficiently "progressive parents," in which owlish children, speaking sententiously and with an idiocy far beyond their years, advise us about the warming of the earth, or health care, or racism, or whatnot. Think of what that means, culturally. We are not talking about fourteen-year-old boys who work in the mines and have some call for our respect. We are talking about children whose practical knowledge is as paltry as their knowledge of poetry, history, geography, mathematics, the sciences, and religion. On what can they base their confidence, these long-faced treble preachers? They base it on what they learn in school—that they are the vanguard of a great future, if only we can all clear their recalcitrant parents out of the way. They are to bring the birch switches home to discipline their parents; the baby beats the nurse, and quite athwart goes all decorum. The politicization of infants, the infantilization of politics.

When Ray Bradbury wrote *Fahrenheit 451*, another novel describing a dystopia of mass stupidity and surveillance, he was not making a prediction either. He was describing what he actually saw in America. His protagonist, Guy Montag, is a "fireman"—note, denizens of the *novus ordo seclorum*, not a "firefighter," since his job is to set fires, not to put them out. Montag is a book burner. Montag's wife, meanwhile, is married to her television. She gapes at her "stories" all day long, yet she cannot relate what is going on in them afterward. She is absorbed into a false world of cheap linguistic and dramatic tricks.

Bradbury insisted that his novel was not about censorship but about how contemporary media have made people shallow and inattentive, squandering their cultural heritage. Shortly after he wrote it, colleges all over the country held their own bonfires, gutting their curricula, completing a destruction that John Dewey and his allies had long before begun, so that now a graduate of Harvard is far more likely to have listened vacantly to a hundred "songs" devoid of melody or sense than to have read a single line of Dante. Too harsh? By far the most popular English course taught at my *mater ferox*, Princeton, is not Shakespeare, as it once was, but Youth Fiction—vampires, adolescent murderers, orgiasts, bad prose, lots of royalties. In a recent semester, more students enrolled in that course than had enrolled in all of Princeton's other English courses combined.

Our Founders believed that a free press was essential for a free society. We believe we have a free press. But what good is nominal freedom—the government does not censor our newspapers—if the writers are liars, or are ill-educated, or feed swill to the populace, or ignore important events because they don't like the people involved or the cause? What happens if the "teaching" of three hundred million Americans rests in the hands of people who give headlines to the latest poster boy for perversion, or to the sleazy habits of a porn girl turned celebrity, or to "scientific" studies about when your "relationship" is going to end, or to the chatter and blather of our current political class, rather than to anything of substance, anything that requires learning, listening, investigating, and thought?

What happens is that the people are swept up into preoccupation with ephemera so that they will buy more of the New and Improved Product, whether it is a news channel, soap, Mr. Smith's candidacy for the Senate, deodorant, the president's council against bullying, pills for old men whose reach exceeds their grasp, a war in a place that most people cannot locate on a globe, advocacy for the computer-surfing poor, a new television show about a detective risen from the dead, toothpaste, or a balanced budget. Everything is political, in the sense that everything is up for public sale, with banners, bullhorns, shiny buttons, and bumper stickers, and nothing is political, in the sense that people do not actually come together in what once were communities to deliberate about the common good.

Stupid Is as Stupid Says

I have often wondered at one of the most peculiar features of our self-styled progressive thought, which is that we take comfort from running down our ancestors. We wish to believe the worst about them and are disappointed or even enraged if someone should suggest to us that our great-grandfathers actually may have loved their wives and, on the whole, gotten along quite well with them, or that children not so long ago could leave school after about eight years, ready to do good work in the world and possessing a surer sense of the English language, of the history of the world and their nation, and of practical mathematics than most of our young people possess when they graduate from high school. It cannot be so! *It must not be so.* The stiff winds of bygone liberty and forgotten knowledge threaten to reduce to sticks and stones our rickety trust in inevitable progress. They encourage us to think and to judge, and we must not do that. The emperor's clothes are splendid, and that's all there is to it.

Let me give an example here of our linguistic degradation—and keep in mind, language is our instrument for thought. If the hammer is made of clay, don't expect to build anything with it. Four hundred

years ago a man named William Shakespeare—almost the last author
from of old who is preserved in our school curricula, like a fly in
amber—wrote a sequence of sonnets exploring the themes of friendship, love, narcissism, age, betrayal, death, and immortality. Like all
such sequences from the time of Dante's *La Vita Nuova*, it is not a
grab bag of poems about this and that, to be dipped into here and
there, at your pleasure. It is itself a coherent work of art, made up of
smaller works of art. It is rather like a work of Renaissance polyph-
ony, in which each "voice" is meant to be heard simultaneously with
the others to produce the strangely harmonious whole. You cannot
read the first sonnet as if it knew nothing of the last sonnet.

Here, for example, is the beloved eighteenth sonnet, which follows a block of seventeen sonnets that urge the young man to whom
the sonnets are addressed to get married and preserve himself by
begetting children. That is one way, says the speaker of the sonnets, to
defeat age and decay and death that come to all. But now the speaker
drops the argument for marriage and children, not to be resumed,
and instead recommends a second way to attain immortality:

Shall I compare thee to a summer's day?
Thou art more lovely and more temperate.
Rough winds do shake the darling buds of May,
And summer's lease hath all too short a date;
Sometime too hot the eye of heaven shines,
And often is his gold complexion dimm'd;
And every fair from fair sometime declines,
By chance or nature's changing course untrimm'd;
But thy eternal summer shall not fade,
Nor lose possession of that fair thou ow'st;
Nor shall death brag thou wander'st in his shade,
When in eternal lines to time thou grow'st:
    So long as men can breathe or eyes can see,
    So long lives this, and this gives life to thee.

There's a lot going on in this sonnet. The speaker makes a strong claim about the life-preserving power of poetry, though, strangely enough, he never identifies the young fellow who is to be made immortal by that poetry, nor does he even trouble to give us those distinguishing features of countenance and personality that would make us feel somehow that we knew him. The work of nature declines as does the summer and the noonday sun, but the speaker will confer upon his friend an everlasting summer—the same speaker who will soon decry his own age and decay, and who will bemoan the fact that the friend's love for him is but temporary, like a lease whose time runs out.

We could go on for many pages examining the subtleties of the poem, noting its beauty, its strange interplay of confidence and sadness, and its many resonances with the sonnets that precede it or follow it. If, then, we are wiser than our forebears, and if we have honed the language into a sharp instrument for thought, even for the expression of wisdom, we should find some evidence of that in poetry written by "famous" poets specifically in response to that poem.

It turns out that a few years ago, *Upstart*, a journal of Renaissance studies published at Clemson University and named for an insult hurled at Shakespeare by his rival poet and playwright Robert Greene, commissioned some contemporary poets to "revise" Shakespeare, writing poems to correspond to each of the sonnets. Some of them are merely strings of words that were left over after the "poet" blacked out most of the words of a sonnet, leaving what is called a "found" poem—a tailbone here, three teeth, and a bit of splintered cranium. Many of them are cheers for sodomy. Most of them have little to do with what Shakespeare was up to in the sequence, or even with what he was up to in the particular sonnet. They are pretty paltry stuff, sometimes obscene, often angry or petulant. Here is the sublingual entry written in response to Sonnet 18. It is titled "Beginning Without a Question":

When I pinned your blue eye. When I collected
my sweat in a jar. When I fingered the scabs

of my knees like a phrenologist. Was it
summer, some wind. Handsome meant

easy to handle then. I was so pliant
there was no plaint yet. Sometime

long ago. So long it became a way to say
goodbye. Clover chains—they cannot

hold you. A frolic of grass. Some wind
meddlesome in your hair. When you toss

back your head. The sun and trees quarrel-
some. The wind a lisping of invisible stars.

Don't ask what those things mean. They don't mean. It is pseudo-poetic gabble, a string of images, meant to express some feeling or other. I suppose that there's some lovemaking going on, though what that has to do with scabs on your own knee, or sweat in a jar, or pinning an eye—what the heck is it to pin an eye?—I don't know, and we are not really supposed to know. It's deep, man, deep. Imagine putting your paint-by-numbers portrait of Mona Lisa next to the one by Leonardo hanging in the Louvre, and imagine that you do not know what a fool you have made of yourself.

The agents of mass stultification have done their work. We have poets who don't understand the artistry of the old masters and artists who have never learned the craft of Titian's portraiture or Rembrandt's shedding of light upon the human face. And we have orators who have not the slightest idea what used to constitute an intelligent political address. Nor will they recover that intelligence, because their audience and they have drunk from the same trough.

As I write these words, the president is declared, by the political class left and right, to be a fine orator. Some of his partisans assert that Barack Obama is the most intelligent man ever to serve as president.

Partisans may be forgiven a degree of hyperbole, but that is absurd. Mr. Obama has never shown any great knowledge of history or of the seminal works of Western civilization. He's not steeped in Aristotle, Cicero, Milton, or Locke; he doesn't take part in those conversations. He could not have attended Paul Elmer More's lecture in Saint Louis without a scorecard to tell the players. His intellectual attainments are modest. He's written about himself with a certain facility, and that's all.

How much we have forgotten! John Adams was a prodigious political philosopher, his library stocked with books in modern and classical languages. His son John Quincy, who as the ex-president in the House of Representatives earned the nickname Old Man Eloquent for his passionate opposition to slavery, worked with the American ambassador to Russia—at age fourteen. Jefferson was a scientist, an inventor, an architect, and the founder of a great university. Madison remains one of the subtlest political writers any nation has produced. Wilson, whose politics I dislike, was a renowned political philosopher and historian, and the president and reformer of Princeton. Hoover was a mining engineer with a degree in geology from Stanford; his wife was the first woman to receive from Stanford that same degree. Together they translated the Renaissance text *De re metallica* as a pastime.

Some of these men were failures as president. Some were successes. Wilson was a success when the country would have been better off had he failed. But none of them possessed the stupidity that Nature alone never bestows. To illustrate, let me compare an "oration" sprung from the habits of mass consumption and intended for mass consumption with an oration that expresses a strong but ordinary intelligence.

Grover Cleveland was a man of solid and sober judgment. He wasn't an electrifying speaker. He never pretended to be. In 1884 he was elected by a slender margin after a bitter fight against the Republican, James G. Blaine. The turning point came when a Republican preacher in New York derided Cleveland's Democrats as the party of "rum, Romanism, and rebellion." Irish Catholics in New York were not pleased. Cleveland, the reformist governor of that state, carried New York by 1,100 votes, and that gave him the presidency.

The preacher's comment reveals the tensions and passions of that age. Temperance societies, and their allies in the woman's suffrage movements, were growing formidable. Anti-Catholic sentiment ran strong, particularly among Republican liberals in the Northeast. Reconstruction of the South had ended by President Hayes's order in 1877, but the memories were fresh and the wounds raw. The people of Vicksburg, which General Grant had starved into submission, would not celebrate Independence Day for decades to come. You could not walk ten miles below the Mason-Dixon line without encountering terrible evidence of the Civil War's destruction.

In that context, at his first inaugural, Cleveland had this to say:

> Today the executive branch of the government is transferred to new keeping. But this is still the government of all the people, and it should be none the less an object of their affectionate solicitude. At this hour *the animosities of political strife, the bitterness of partisan defeat, and the exultation of partisan triumph* [emphasis mine] should be supplanted by an ungrudging acquiescence in the popular will, and a sober, conscientious concern for the general weal. Moreover, if from this hour we cheerfully and honestly abandon all sectional prejudice and distrust, and determine, with manly confidence in one another, to work out harmoniously the achievement of our national destiny, we shall deserve to realize all the benefits which our happy form of government can bestow.

That is the speech of a sensible man. Cleveland could engage in a flourish when he wanted to, which wasn't often. There was nothing florid about what he said. He called no attention to himself. He did not congratulate the people for having elected him. He called for sobriety and amity, even from the millions of people who had personal reasons for enmity. Their reasons were not abstract. They could look out of their windows and see those reasons: a demolished house, a road torn up, a farm thicketed with thorns and thistles, a family cemetery, with crosses to mark a father, two brothers, a son, and children whose deaths were brought on by hunger and exposure.

Now President Obama, who entered office in the midst of a recession—recessions do occur—and not shortly after a civil war:

> On this day, we gather because we have chosen hope over fear, unity of purpose over conflict and discord. On this day, we come to proclaim an end to the petty grievances and false promises, the recriminations and worn-out dogmas that for far too long have strangled our politics.

Notice the graceless move. Nearly half of the voting public *did not choose* President Obama. But he implies that a vote for him was a vote for hope; presumably, a vote for his opponent was a vote for fear. Our opponents suffered the compulsions of that disreputable emotion. Our opponents suffered a moral and psychological trouble. The pronoun *we*, then, is exclusive: we, the ones who think rightly.

All the nouns are vague. What conflict? What discord, exactly? Cleveland acknowledged "sectional prejudice" and "the animosities of political strife," just as any sensible Christian will frankly acknowledge his proneness to sin and as any honest man will acknowledge that he does not know everything and sometimes will be blinded by his passions.

President Obama, by contrast, does not think that the condition of frail man applies to all parties at all times. Apparently, until the day he stood to take the oath of office, American politics had been a matter of "petty grievances" and "false promises." If to appraise your sins without mercy is to approach the threshold of moral liberty, then to fail to appraise them, and instead to attribute sins to some vague others outside, or in the past, is to remain a prisoner. It is what Jesus suggests when he notes the terrible irony of the hypocrite who says to his brother, "Let me take the speck out of your eye," when all along there is a plank in his own. Jesus does not mean that every man's eye is clear. He means to have us look first to ourselves and our failings, which will require a good deal of time and trouble. Then we may eventually see well enough to take the speck out of our brother's eye.

But none of that honesty is here in evidence. It cannot be. It would never thrive in the politics of compulsion, which depends upon a continually instigated sense of urgency. If you take the long view of human history, the next politician on the scene need not surprise you, nor will that politician have to persuade you that he is a savior, the herald of a new world. All he needs to do is to assure you of his love for your country, his honesty and diligence, and his good sense. We can greet him with that healthiest of responses, an approving nod and a yawn, while we return to the real business of life.

Not now, though. No one can be made to feel *compelled* to buy a car that is merely *all right*. It must be stupendous. It must cause lascivious girls to drape their slender arms about your neck. It must, with the aid of computer-generated images, porn for car sales, sail over the Snake River Canyon. No one can say, "Elect me, and I promise nothing other than honesty, modesty in what we will attempt to do, and the grace to defer to you to deal with your problems by your best lights." Elect a demagogue, a people flatterer, a heaven promiser? We will not elect anyone *unless* he is such. We *must* fall for the words that call for an automatic response, lest we think.

What about the writing? Cleveland's sentences are long but balanced. The words and ideas are in harmony. Nothing is chosen for mere effect. But what on earth can Mr. Obama mean by a "worn-out dogma" "strangling our politics"? I imagine a black-hooded Dogma, its bony fingers round the neck of poor Politics, who must have an iron neck anyhow, because this is a strangling that's gone on for "far too long." Most stranglings take only a minute.

Mr. Obama may have been absent on the day when his high school teacher warned against heedless forays into the Land of Metaphor:

> The words [of the oath of office] have been spoken during rising tides of prosperity and the still waters of peace. Yet, every so often the oath is taken amidst gathering clouds and raging

storms. At these moments, America has carried on not simply because of the skill or vision of those in high office, but because We the People have remained faithful to the ideals of our forebears, and true to our founding documents.

Yes, that's four weather clichés in a row. It's the work of a good high school sophomore circa 2000. I have beside me now a high school grammar text whose authors note that some slovenly writers use "will" for the first person to express futurity when they should use "shall." Needless to say, that text was written a long time ago. It is filled with hundreds of samples of good and great writing, from Shakespeare, Addison, Johnson, Bunyan, Milton, Pope, Dickens, Charlotte Brontë, Whittier, Emerson, the Bible, and so forth. Its authors would never call the passage above slovenly. They would be laughing or weeping too hard to do so.

Laughing, perhaps, until the condescension pulled them up short. During times of trouble, the spanking new leader says, America has survived *not simply* because of the skill or vision of national politicians. In one breath, the people are flattered, because they too—who would have thought it?—have contributed to the success of the nation, and they are rendered infantile, for they have always needed and always will need the "skill or vision of those in high office." Then comes the obligatory importation of the first words of the Constitution and the nod to "our founding documents," which Mr. Obama himself has dismissed as outdated.

It is a commercial for a national hormone pill.

This, by contrast, is President Cleveland placing himself in the company of ordinary people:

But he who takes the oath today to preserve, protect, and defend the Constitution of the United States only assumes the solemn obligation which every patriotic citizen—on the farm, in the workshop, in the busy marts of trade, and everywhere—should share with him. The Constitution which prescribes his oath, my countrymen, is yours; the government you have chosen him to administer for a time is yours; the suffrage which executes the will of freemen is yours; the laws and the entire scheme of our civil rule, from the town meeting to the state capitals and the national capital, is yours. Your every voter, as surely as your Chief Magistrate, under the same high sanction, though in a different sphere, exercises a public trust.

Notice that Cleveland had a modest and clearheaded view of who he was and what he was commissioned to do. He had been chosen to "administer" the national government "for a time." There was no sense of a revolution in human affairs. Cleveland insisted upon the dignity and proper duties of the other polities, implying a just restraint upon his own office. He would, he said, be guided by "a careful observance of the distinction between the powers granted to the federal government and those reserved to the states or to the people."

Obama makes no such distinctions and does not recognize those other polities. Instead he indulges an exaggerated sense of his capacities—pardonable in a boy, embarrassing in a man:

Starting today, we must pick ourselves up, dust ourselves off, and begin again the work of remaking America.

For everywhere we look, there is work to be done. The state of our economy calls for action, bold and swift. And we will act not only to create new jobs but to lay a new foundation for growth. We will build the roads and bridges, the electric grids and digital lines that feed our commerce and bind us together. We will restore science to its rightful place and wield technology's wonders to raise health care's quality and lower its costs. We will harness the sun and the winds and the soil to fuel our cars and run our factories. And we will transform our schools and colleges and universities to meet the demands of a new age.

Heaping triteness upon triteness, the perorator says "we"—meaning his government—"will build the roads and bridges," as if we have been riding mules along deer paths in the woods. "We" will "restore science to its rightful place," implying that scientific research and discovery have not been going on all along. The "rightful place" then must mean "its rightful preeminence over all other human concerns," so that ordinary people again will have no recourse to common sense but will have to wait hat in hand for the "scientist" to decide every human question. That enthronement will allow us to wield wonders, and we can almost hear the threat, *whether you people like it or not.* We will "harness" the sun, with a long lasso, and even harness the soil—how do you harness soil?—to fuel our cars, *thump thump.*

Far from acknowledging any limits upon the executive, he promises to "transform our schools and colleges and universities." What does that mean? I don't know. What's the "new age," which sophomores have been invoking ever since there were freshmen, and which Obama invokes twice? I don't know. Whatever that new age is, it is coming, again whether we like it or not. It is inexorable. The repeated *we will* means *you must, or else.*

And then there's the quotation. The sophomore mounts to the podium. "As Robert Frost once said, 'I took the road less traveled by,'" and eyes roll heavenward and the sensible teacher stifles a groan. If you use a quotation, it had better be apropos. If it is a quotation from a sacred text, it should be held as determinative, not wrested from its place to serve purposes alien to its meaning.

Grover Cleveland had the sense or the modesty to understand the point. Consider how he described the foreign policy he would pursue, a policy generally observed through the nineteenth century, and one with much to recommend it:

> It is the policy of independence, favored by our position and
> defended by our known love of justice and by our own power.
> It is the policy of peace suitable to our interests. It is the policy

of neutrality, rejecting any share in foreign broils and ambitions upon other continents and repelling their intrusion here. It is the policy of Monroe, and of Washington, and of Jefferson—"Peace, commerce, and honest friendship with all nations; entangling alliance with none."

The parallelism built to the climax provided by the quotation, as Cleveland invoked the revered names of three of his predecessors, leading with Monroe, whose doctrine he expressed with admirable economy in the phrase "repelling their intrusion here."

And now Barack Obama:

We remain a young nation, but in the words of Scripture, the time has come to set aside childish things.

We aren't young, but set that aside. Why has he quoted Saint Paul? Paul is talking about the maturity of the Christian soul, which desires to see God not simply as through a glass, darkly, but face to face. What can that have to do with a change of political administrations? Is Mr. Obama suggesting that the whole prior history of America has been childish? What does it mean? We must not probe too closely. It's just a quotation, tossed in to impress the freshman girl up front. Cleveland was a man speaking to men. Our politicians now are teen idols performing before their groupies. That's the more innocent interpretation. The more sinister is simply this. If you revere anything from the past, you must be swept aside. Board the train, or be run over. *You must.*

The Idiot Proper

Odysseus the wanderer is seated at table with King Alcinous and his queen and the nobility of Phaeacia. He is describing his adventures after he set forth for home from Troy. And now he and his men have put ashore on the island of the Cyclopes, gigantic man-eating monsters about whom most people remember only one thing: a Cyclops has one great eye in the center of his forehead.

That single eye, the reader will recall, comes into play in the adventure. Had the Cyclops drowsed off in a drunken stupor with two eyes rather than one, Odysseus and his men would not have been able to blind him, burning the eye's jelly to the roots with their fire-hardened stake. But had the Cyclops been able to see out of two eyes—that is, with the depth of truly human judgment—he would not have lived the life he did, so that when he cried out, using the phony name Odysseus had given him, "No-man is hurting me," his neighbors would not have scoffed, telling him that if No-man was hurting him, what was he complaining about? And had the Cyclops honored the gods, he and Odysseus would have enjoyed a most fascinating conversation. But the Cyclops, who can speak, and who has real affections, is still not human. He *should have been* human, perhaps, but is not.

That is because the Cyclops already lives the life of what the Greeks considered the "idiot"—literally, someone who does not consider the common good, someone self-absorbed, aloof, contemptuous of the community. So does Odysseus describe the life of the Single-Eyed before we even meet the ogre with the bad table manners:

> We sailed hence, always in much distress, till we came to the land of the lawless and inhuman Cyclopes. Now the Cyclopes neither plant nor plough, but trust in providence, and live on such wheat, barley, and grapes as grow wild without any kind of tillage, and their wild grapes yield them wine as the sun and the rain may grow them. They have no laws nor assemblies of the people, but live in caves on the tops of high mountains; each is lord and master in his family, and they take no account of their neighbours.

Odysseus appraises the island in the Cyclopian harbor with the eye of a farmer, a vine grower, a sailor, a civilized man:

It is over-run with wild goats, that breed there in great numbers and are never disturbed by foot of man... nor yet again is it
ever ploughed or fed down, but it lies a wilderness untilled and
unsown from year to year, and has no living thing upon it but
only goats. For the Cyclopes have no ships, nor yet shipwrights
who could make ships for them; they cannot therefore go from
city to city, or sail over the sea to one another's country as people who have ships can do; if they had had these they would
have colonized the island, for it is a very good one, and would
yield everything in due season. There are meadows that in some
places come right down to the sea shore, well watered and full of
luscious grass; grapes would do there excellently; there is level
land for ploughing, and it would always yield heavily at harvest time, for the soil is deep. There is a good harbour where no
cables are wanted, nor yet anchors, nor need a ship be moored,
but all one has to do is to beach one's vessel and stay there till the
wind becomes fair for putting out to sea again.

Finally, when Odysseus actually meets Polyphemus of the single
eye, he begs for hospitality, appealing to the gods above. Whereupon
Polyphemus replies:

"Stranger," said he, "you are a fool, or else you know nothing of
this country. Talk to me, indeed, about fearing the gods or shun-
ning their anger? We Cyclopes do not care about Jove or any of
your blessed gods, for we are ever so much stronger than they.
I shall not spare either yourself or your companions out of any
regard for Jove, unless I am in the humor for doing so."

At which point he dashes out the brains of two of Odysseus's men and
has them for dinner.

Let us try to put Homer's insights together. It is subhuman, it is
"idiotic," to give way to your baser desires, here shown by the ogre's
excess in food and drink. It is subhuman, it is "idiotic," to live only for

the selfish pleasures of the day, taking no thought for the morrow. It is subhuman, it is the mark of the essential idiot, to live by and for oneself, shrugging away the gods, and having neighbors only by physical proximity, not by bonds of duty or love of one's home and native land. The Cyclops is most like the suitors who have besieged Odysseus's home, courting his wife, plotting the murder of his son, guzzling his wine, and feasting upon his flocks and herds. For in the twenty years since Odysseus was compelled to leave his home, the men of Ithaca had not met once in assembly, until the king's son Telemachus called them to account for their negligence, because they had allowed their sons to ravish Odysseus's estate.

What Homer could never have foreseen is the double idiocy into which we now educate our children. We have what look like our equivalent to the Greek "assemblies"; we can watch them on cable television, as long as one can endure them. For they are charades of political action. They concern themselves constantly, insufferably, about every tiniest feature of human existence, but without slow deliberation, without balance, without any commitment to the difficult virtues. We do not have men locked in intellectual battle with other men, worthy opponents both, as Thomas Paine battled with John Dickinson, or Daniel Webster with Robert Hayne. We have men strutting and mugging for women nagging and bickering. We have the sputters of what used to be language, "tweets," expressions of something less than opinion. It is the urge to join—something, anything—while remaining aloof from the people who live next door, whose names we do not know. Aristotle once wrote that youths should not study politics, because they had not the wealth of human experience to allow for it; all would become for them abstract and theoretical, like mathematics, which the philosopher said was more suitable for them. He concluded that men should begin to study politics at around the age of forty.

Whether that wisdom would help us now, I don't know.

5

Lusts, Not Love

The Itch

A young man in Vienna is being led to prison. He has broken a law that had fallen into disuse: he has gotten his betrothed with child. The Duke of Vienna, a mild and tolerant man, allowed the laws to grow musty and has arranged for a subterfuge he hopes will remedy the ill. He has given out that he has left the city on national business, leaving the commonwealth in the charge of a severe young subordinate, Angelo. That man is one who "scarce confesses that his blood flows," or so it seems. He is not likely to look indulgently upon sins of the flesh. The penalty for the young man, Claudio, is death.

Claudio's rakish friend Lucio accosts him along the way and asks, "Whence comes this restraint?" He means the shackles, but Claudio interprets the question existentially:

From too much liberty, my Lucio, liberty:
As surfeit is the father of much fast,
So every scope by the immoderate use
Turns to restraint. Our natures do pursue,
Like rats that ravin down their proper bane,
A thirsty evil; and when we drink we die.

For liberty, read license. The metaphor that Shakespeare uses here, in *Measure for Measure*, is powerful and disturbing. People who surrender to license, particularly sexual license, are like rats devouring their "proper bane," rat poison. The more the rat eats, the more it has to eat—it ravins it down, greedily devouring the deadly stuff, which makes it grow thirstier and thirstier, and when it drinks, it dies.

Shakespeare was no hater of the flesh. But despite his merriment with what man and wife do when the guests are gone and the children are asleep—or maybe it's what allowed him to be so merry—he had a high view of the holiness of marriage, and he never allowed sins against the marriage bed to go unpunished. Perhaps the most painful example of it comes from *King Lear*. In a typically understated opening scene, the Duke of Gloucester introduces his illegitimate son, Edmund, with the following words, wavering between shame and pride:

> I have, sir, a son by order of law, some year
> elder than this, who yet is no dearer in my account:
> though this knave came something saucily into the
> world before he was sent for, yet was his mother
> fair; there was good sport at his making, and the
> whoreson must be acknowledged.

What the whoreson Edmund makes of his hole-and-corner begetting we see in a later scene. He forges a letter in his brother's handwriting, purporting to seek means to do away with Gloucester so that the two sons can enjoy the estate without having to wait for old age to do its slow work. This, to get rid of the noble lad; he can deal with the father later.

Gloucester, dismayed by the letter and by the king's banishment of his most loving daughter, thinks that the whole world is breaking up before their eyes:

> These late eclipses in the sun and moon portend
> no good to us: though the wisdom of nature can

reason it thus and thus, yet nature finds itself
scourged by the sequent effects: love cools,
friendship falls off, brothers divide; in
cities, mutinies; in countries, discord; in
palaces, treason; and the bond cracked 'twixt son
and father.

When Gloucester leaves, shaking his head, Edmund speaks to the audience directly, in contempt:

This is the excellent foppery of the world, that,
when we are sick in fortune—often the surfeit
of our own behavior—we make guilty of our
disasters the sun, the moon, and the stars: as
if we were villains by necessity; fools by
heavenly compulsion; knaves, thieves, and
treachers, by spherical predominance; drunkards,
liars, and adulterers, by an enforced obedience of
planetary influence; and all that we are evil in,
by a divine thrusting on: an admirable evasion
of whoremaster man, to lay his goatish
disposition to the charge of a star!

For the sun, the moon, and the stars, substitute anything you like, anything that will deflect attention from your evil ways to something you cannot change: your parents' income, your psychological constitution, your ancestry, the television, the Internet. In a single breathtaking contradiction, proclaim your liberty to do the evil you please *and your having been compelled to it* by the way you were born or how you were raised. Say in one sentence that you are free and that you can do no otherwise.

Well then, Gloucester, with a smack for the "sport" of adultery, your bastard son will use your loyalty to King Lear to betray you to your enemies. What those enemies will do to you is well summed up by the good son Edgar, speaking to Edmund after he has given him his death wound:

> The gods are just, and of our pleasant vices
> Make instruments to plague us:
> The dark and vicious place where thee he got
> Cost him his eyes.

It is by no means an isolated incident in Shakespeare's plays. In *Othello*, were it not for the affair between the slick-talking Michael Cassio and the whore Bianca (who wants him to marry her, while Cassio laughs at her behind her back), Iago would never have been able to persuade the Moor that his wife had been unfaithful to him. The callow young Bertram, in *All's Well That Ends Well*, tries to debauch a young woman, but the lawful wife he has rejected prevents it by taking the girl's place, unbeknownst to the boy. He is subjected to public humiliation. The adulterous love of King Edward for Jane Shore gives his villainous brother Richard a way to pretend alliance with Lord Hastings (also in bed with Mistress Shore), whom he will later send to his death. Romeo's haste and Mark Antony's obsession prove their undoing. Queen Margaret's adulterous affair with Suffolk helps to plunge England into a long civil war.

And male chastity? Some people treat it as a jest, as if men were not supposed to be able to control themselves. Compelled, you see. So Ariosto winks at us when his hero, Ruggiero, saves the naked Angelica from being eaten by a phallic sea monster, spirits her away on his flying horse, and then, well, forgets about his fiancée and puts in at the nearest island, trying so hard to take off his clothes that he buttons two buttons for every one he loosens. Fielding will champion the unusual virtue of his Joseph Andrews ("Did ever mortal hear of a man's virtue?" exclaims the widow Lady Booby, fairly out of her mind with lust for him), but with a faint intimation, now and then, of absurdity.

Such an intimation is not to be found from the genius of Shakespeare. In *Macbeth*, when Malcolm, legitimate heir to the usurped throne of Scotland, tests Macduff's loyalty, he pretends to all manner of vices, including "voluptuousness":

Your wives, your daughters,
Your matrons and your maids, could not fill up
The cistern of my lust, and my desire
All continent impediments would o'erbear
That did oppose my will.

He is not talking about rape. He is talking about fornication. King Juan Carlos of Spain, a biographer has written, bedded some fifteen hundred women, and that has somehow not earned him a name for dissipation and vice. But Macduff does not laugh at Malcolm's confession. He admits that lust is a "tyranny" and has been the undoing of many a king. But he tries to make the best of a bad situation, noting that in Scotland "we have willing dames enough." So in Spain too, apparently.

Malcolm is not so. "I am yet / Unknown to woman," says the young man, and in the same speech he claims that he has never been forsworn and never broken faith. "What I am truly," he says, "Is thine and my poor country's to command." He is not the only high-minded lad in Shakespeare. In *The Winter's Tale*, we meet a young prince, Florizel, who is courting the daughter of a rich shepherd. They are dressed up in masquerade to celebrate a sheep-shearing feast. The lass, Perdita, worrying that Florizel's father will find them out, wonders what he would say if he saw Florizel in such garb. Florizel replies that the gods themselves have taken on "the shapes of beasts" to compass their loves, yet there is a crucial and noble difference:

Their transformations
Were never for a piece of beauty rarer,
Nor in a way so chaste, since my desires
Run not before mine honor, nor my lusts
Burn hotter than my faith.

He does not say that his desire for Perdita is cool. It burns hot, and all the hotter *because* of his strong faith, *because* he will not sully her cleanness. As the poet Spenser says, they who are moved only by lust have "dunghill minds." Their fire does not aspire to the heavens. Lust is the fire that dampens, the license that fetters.

Perhaps the finest affirmation of male chastity, though, is to be found in *The Tempest*—the finest because it is expressed in terms that frankly acknowledge the fire of eros and the longing for the wedding night. Prospero is giving his daughter, Miranda, in marriage to the prince Ferdinand. But he warns the youngsters against untimeliness. In its failure to wait for the proper time, unchastity is a sin against nature, a sin that sows the marriage bed with weeds and brings forth no fruitful harvest. Ferdinand's response to Prospero is manly, forthright, and chaste:

> As I hope
> For quiet days, fair issue, and long life,
> With such love as 'tis now, the murkiest den,
> The most opportune place, the strong'st suggestion.
> Our worser genius can, shall never melt
> Mine honor into lust, to take away
> The edge of that day's celebration
> When I shall think or Phoebus' steeds are founder'd
> Or Night kept chain'd below.

"Fairly spoke," replies Prospero. "Sit then and talk with her; she is thine own."

Virtue, Maker of Freedom

What kind of liberty does the virtue of chastity embody? Let's turn to John Milton, our great poetic champion of both chastity and liberty.

When we first enter Eden in *Paradise Lost*, we encounter a great riot of beauty: lush grapevines hanging over grottoes and heavy with fruit, grassy meadows full of browsing cattle and sheep, streams splashing their way over the rocks, and flowers pouring forth at the bidding of "Nature boon," who showers her gifts in abundance.

There is nothing either automatic or artificially restrained in this Nature. Eve will observe that although she and Adam spend much of the morning and the afternoon at their pleasant labor, tending the plants to make their garden beautiful and comfortable, the flowers and vines *grow by restraint.* That is not just an odd feature of the flora of Eden. It is a law of created being. I become greater not by attempting to violate the character of my human nature but by observing it, building it up, warning it against sliding back into the automatic reactions of a beast or against pretending that I am an angel or a god. The farmer who will not till in straight furrows must go hungry. The carpenter who will not respect the nature of pine or oak will find the rain dripping on his head at night. Deny yourself a trivial good to seek the greater. Prune the tree to gather more fruit.

Milton expected his readers to understand that principle. To acknowledge that God is God, which is all that the prohibition against eating of the forbidden tree means, is the easy and yet all-important "restraint" that causes those who observe it to grow. But Satan, "through all restraint broke loose," has winged his way to the new-created world to tempt the free man and woman to their imprisonment. He will do that, of course, by holding forth a delusive license, what Whittaker Chambers called the dogma of man's second oldest faith: Ye shall be as gods.

It is bitterly ironic that the fiend who poses as a liberator should see liberal Nature in all her beauty and should hate it all the more for its liberality. He sees "undelighted all delight," and then he comes upon a sight that saddens him to the core of his being:

> Two of far nobler shape, erect and tall,
> Godlike erect, with native honor clad
> In naked majesty seemed lords of all,

And worthy seemed: for in their looks divine
The image of their glorious Maker shone:
Truth, wisdom, sanctitude severe and pure,
Severe, but in true filial freedom placed.

Adam and Eve are both naked and clad: their innocence and their honor are a robe of majesty, and they need no other. They are free to be naked, without the "troublesome disguises which we wear," because they are pure.

Milton understood that chastity is not the same as abstinence, just as freedom is not the same as permission. Adam and Eve are chaste, and they *do not* abstain from the "rites mysterious" of wedded love. What they do is not merely permissible. It is creative, holy, blessed by God. That is why their nightly bower is a sacred place where none of the lowly animals will go, "such was their awe of man." They enter it after prayer, hand in hand. Theirs is not "casual fruition" but the consummation of their love as embodied souls made by the God of love. They do not use each other as instruments to scratch an itch. Chastity is the virtue of reverence for sexual being, male and female, in oneself and in all other persons.

This reverence implies an illuminating realism with regard to sex. What Pope John Paul II called the "nuptial meaning of the body" is powerfully evident to anyone who sees a husband and wife walking together, hands joined, her head perhaps leaning upon his shoulder. This sense of fitness precedes a child's awareness of the details of sexual intercourse, but it is founded upon that reality, for the "mysterious parts," as Milton calls them, are made for one another. I can breathe on my own, digest food on my own, think thoughts on my own. The one bodily thing I cannot do on my own is the most time-transcending and creative thing of all: the child-making thing. Only a man and a woman together, in true sexual intercourse—that is, the interactive congress of the sexes as such, male and female—can do that.

Here we stand on the shores of a vast and life-giving but also perilous sea. Sex is the first thing we notice about someone and the last thing we forget. In social situations it never quite fades from our awareness. We understand that the man is *for the woman*, as the woman is *for the man*. This *being-for* is marked in the differences themselves. In husband and wife, these differences are for completion, as Genesis suggests and as Milton makes clear, in the scene when Adam pursues the newly created Eve:

> To give thee being I lent
> Out of my side to thee, nearest my heart,
> Substantial life, to have thee by my side
> Henceforth an individual solace dear;
> Part of my soul I seek thee, and thee claim
> My other half.

Adam is not just talking about the pleasure of friendship or the enlargement of the heart and the mind gained by social interchange generally. He is talking of something new in the world: the literally "individual" solace of marriage, wherein the man and the woman become one flesh, never, without grave sin, to be put asunder.

Man is a social being; he casts bridges over the rifts that separate one person from another. But the union of man and woman is more splendid by far than those ordinary bridges. In it alone do we unite with a different kind of human being altogether, a person who sows the seed, which a woman can never do, or a person who is the field wherein the seed and the egg bear fruit, which a man can never be. It requires the most radical surrender of self. I do not simply mean that the man and woman have certain feelings. I mean that the man, precisely as a man, gives himself entirely in the act of sexual congress to the woman, who gives herself in return, as a woman. The very act cries out: "I was made for you," meaning not just, "I make you happy," or even, "I will always be with you," but rather, "Everything that I am, in all the reality of my sex, belongs to you, is yours by right, because with you its meaning, biological and personal, is consummated."

Unlike mere abstinence, then, chastity is ineluctably social. It colors all our relations with men and women, because it recognizes men and women and reveres them as sexual beings. Every man, married or not, is the sort of being oriented toward fatherhood, as every woman is oriented toward motherhood. I'm not saying that every man will sire a child; nor will every woman bear a child. A priest may be a spiritual father; a nun may be a spiritual mother.

And we can draw a corollary from the being-for that is inscribed in each sex. Animals reproduce; only man, in the act of love, knows that he is doing what his parents did, and what his children may do in turn. The meaning of the act transcends the moment just insofar as the man and woman are open to that fact and all that it implies. It is a logical and psychological contradiction to say, "I give myself entirely to you," while saying, "I deny you the fullness of my sexual being, and the heritage of the generations that I bear within me." That is to treat a man or a woman as somewhat less than a man or a woman: as male and female givers of pleasure, as scratching posts.

C. S. Lewis shrewdly noted that the first casualty of a misplaced exaltation of eros is eros itself. He found that wisdom in the works of the great medieval and Renaissance poets: Chrétien de Troyes, Jean de Meun, Dante, Chaucer, Tasso, Sidney, Spenser, Shakespeare, and Milton. Their wisdom confirmed what he saw with his eyes, and what we can see with ours if we would open them. For the deadening is there to be seen. Where chastity is not honored, people lose their reverence for the sexes, and with that reverence they lose the dimension of depth in their sexual encounters. These tend to be loveless and joyless, disappointing, even perfunctory. The simple pleasures of sexuality are lost.

A lad and a lass cannot flirt innocently without the shadow of a sexual liaison falling over the act. They are "free" to fornicate, but that very license cramps them and everyone else. The stakes are raised too high. If a boy says to a girl, "Would you like to go to a movie with me?" she must think beyond the movie—far beyond. Knowing that this is so, the boy does not trouble to ask her in the first place, unless he too intends the bed. You cannot begin an ordinary business in a land where graft, promise-breach, adulteration, and cheating prevail. Your nominal freedom to do so is inconsequential. You may as well proclaim yourself free to walk down an alley in a crime-ridden street.

The dash, the pursuit, the courtship, the sending of poems, the singing of songs, the high-hearted pleasure of a smile, or the touch of a hand—all these are dulled. Nor is the damage limited to relations between the sexes. Without the freedom granted by chastity *among members of the same sex*, the boy cannot enjoy the foolish pleasures of boyhood of old. If you look at old photographs of high school football or baseball teams, you will see the boys fairly hanging all over one another; that physical expression of affection is possible only because reverence for male sexual being clears room for it. Boys are for girls: that is that. If one were to intrude upon this picture of camaraderie and say, "I feel a sexual desire for you," that would do violence to the maleness of the boys. It would be a subtle attempt to subvert their confidence that they are husbands-to-be or fathers-to-be. It would force their attention back upon themselves. They must conceive of their maleness in the severely restricted sense that they possess a certain sort of body, without considering what that body is for. It would dampen philia with eros, and then would corrupt eros, replacing it with a kind of mutual autoeroticism.

Itching Powder for Sale

EPIC SEX!
GET IT, GIVE IT, AND GET IT AGAIN!
—*From the cover of a recent issue of* Cosmopolitan *magazine*

The magazine cover splays the truth out naked before our eyes. There's no person there, no one who needs love, no one sad or shy or confused. There's no warmth, not even in sin. Human eros, as opposed to the urges of a brute beast, bears the intimations of eternity, of a love that does not fail. But this does not rise to the level of eros. It hardly rises to the level of natural hunger. The degenerate rich in the days of the Roman Empire would binge and purge and binge, for a sickly pleasure in eating and for distraction from the emptiness of their lives. The cover encourages the same bingeing and purging, get and give and get...what? Some undefined object. "Pick me up, open me," it whispers, wheedling. "I hide the secret of *epic sex*!" The adjective, once filled with literary and human meaning, is empty, to be filled with that subhunger, that terrible desire for something, anything, to desire.

That is what *prurience* is all about. It is, literally, the instigation of an *itch*. It doesn't have to be about sex, but in our mass marketing, sex is the most common virus for the inception and the spread of the rash. The itch brings no joy. We know that when we are scratching some scrofulous dermatitis, we'd be better off not scratching. But we can't help ourselves. To think about the itch, without scratching, would drive us mad. It is why Dante, cunning psychologist, punished the petty bunko artists with a never-subsiding itch, the sufferers raking their flesh as if they were scraping the scales off a pike. They feel a ferocious moment's relief, burning in frustration. The prurient cannot move an inch without the tickle, the prick, the bristle.

He says, "I won't scratch that itch! I won't think about it. I'll count to ten." But none of those tricks work. It is the colossal failure of some (not all) calls to abstinence, when there is nothing grand or beautiful beyond to stir a noble human longing. The call to abstinence, detached from the deepest human realities, is nothing more than a call *not to scratch the itch*. It acknowledges the itch. It reminds us of the itch. It allows the itch to creep. It permits the prurience of magazines, library books, advertising campaigns, politicians, video games, all the little spikes and prickles of a consumptive economy, coughing and coughing. Then it says, "In all these other ways you may debase yourself. You may scratch here, here, and here, yes, a little to the left, ah yes, but not *here*."

Nor are our schools any refuge. They are the insanatoria where the law of the itch is taught. They lace their textbooks with the oil of poison ivy. "Protect yourself from these diseases," our children are advised, because they *must yield to the disease they have already caught.* There are human choices only around the edges of the rash— *how* to scratch, not whether. That partly explains curricular choices for high school literature courses. Where the itch has set in, it must be scratched; where it has not set in, it must be introduced. It also explains choices for stocking the school libraries with "young adult" books about vampires, zombies, spicy fornicators, and admirable murderers in this or that miserable dystopia. The school snuggles up to the covers of *Self, Glamour, Elle, Maxim, Us, Scrape, Rip, Itch.*

I understand the challenge the few smooth-skinned teachers face. The children have been itching and scratching for years. They skitter from video game to video game. They don't read. If they do, it's puerile websites, or sniggering celebrity magazines, or "novels" whose dialogues range from the grunt to the sneer. These young people are precociously senescent. They cannot be moved by the feelings of Mr. Knightley for Emma. They need scratching. And unwise or prurient teachers oblige. Hence the choice for "controversial" or "relevant" works to spur real "discussion," because only a text seasoned with obscenities and profanities, or cruelty, or perversion, will do. That is called being on the "cutting edge": the scratching edge.

The itch is but the poor, measly counterfeit of the *quest*: the liberating gift of oneself to find something of incomparable worth and beauty.

Music and the Itch

Like dew on the gowan lying
Is the fa' o' her fairy feet,
And like winds in summer sighing
Her voice is low and sweet.
Her voice is low and sweet,
And she's a' the world to me,

And for bonnie Annie Laurie
I would lay me doon an' dee.
    —*From the old Scottish ballad "Annie Laurie"*

What I want is whatcha got
And whatcha got is what I want . . .
What a girl wants, what a girl needs
Somebody sensitive, crazy, sexy, cool like you
What a girl wants, what a girl needs . . .
Ya let a girl know how much ya care about her, I swear
    —*From a hit "song" on the planet Obsessus*

I have before me a copy of a Community Song Book, printed in Canada and falling apart from long and constant use. It is filled with *folk songs*—that is, songs beloved by the people and passed down from one generation to the next *because* they were beloved. There are anthems: "O Canada," its lyrics unexpurgated by the thought police, and the boisterous "Rule, Britannia" and "The Marseillaise." There are sweet love songs, like "Annie Laurie" and "Loch Lomond" and "Juanita." There are gently mournful songs of sorrow and loss; silly playful songs; songs from the American South, from Hawaii ("Aloha Oe"), from all over Europe.

Some of the lyrics were written by poets of the first rank: Ben Jonson's "Drink to Me Only with Thine Eyes," Robert Burns's "Auld Lang Syne." Others were written by some unknown poet or were like sudden springs bubbling up out of the common heritage of music. The melodies also ranged far and wide, from the haunting minor key melodies of the negro spiritual, to military fanfares, to the simple bumptiousness of comic songs ("Old Dan Tucker"). Dvorak and Schubert find a place beside Stephen Foster and that busy fellow, Composer Unknown.

The foreword to the book says there is nothing so vital for bringing a community together as song. The music is scored for four-part harmony, so that really experienced community singers could venture forth into the fine complexities of soprano, alto, tenor, and bass.

The people, then, would experience the music not only by hearing but also by singing, and not in unison but in *union*. "Various voices make the sweeter song," says Dante, celebrating the *differences* in rank among the blessed souls in heaven. And so, too, in the choirs that used this book, young and old would find their harmonies, boys and women and men, and all classes of people. That explains, too, the prominence of the most important kind of song in the book, the hymns: "Nearer, My God, to Thee." For people are truly united only from above, never from below.

It's with a shock, then, that we turn to the lyrics of our planet Obsessus, sublingual coos and grunts, without coherence, sweetness, grace, solemnity, mirth, or humor. They are entirely focused on the self, valuing the "you" only as a provider of commodities. What a girl wants, what a girl needs. Here on Obsessus, not many people play musical instruments. We don't have community song, because we have no community, and we have no song. We don't actually *listen to music*, although we believe we do. We do not sit quietly and attend to it, as one might attend to Dvorak's *New World Symphony*, which Dvorak could write only because he had visited America, when there was an America, and gotten to know her people, and heard their songs. We play it as noise to accompany something else we are doing, quite often something that also bears the character of a compulsion—work at a dull job, "hooking up" with someone whose name we haven't caught, jogging to lose those last five pounds or trim off that last inch of the commercially decried "unwanted belly fat," cramming food or facts or forms to fill out.

On Obsessus we use "music," a canned array of sounds, as a means to scratch an itch. It's a mechanical rake on the back of one's chair or brain. The use of the music reflects both its subject and its form. These are extraordinarily narrow. They cram those who cram into the tight anxious space of narcissistic self-inspection, but never *introspection*.

Which brings us back up to earth, the planet where we used to dwell, whose night skies, unlike those on Obsessus, are open to the heavens. The man who first sang of Annie Laurie held that young lady in his mind as the epitome of beauty. He remembers himself only in relation to her. But on Obsessus the singer remembers the lover only in relation to the self. The old Scotsman can see her fair hands and her neck; he can recall her gentle voice. He is far away from her; he may never see her again. But for her, for bonnie Annie Laurie, he would lay himself down and die. He doesn't intend that as a boast, but in that lovely final line—and its surprising full-octave leap, on the syllable *lay*—he rises in our esteem, for his devotion and humility.

There's all the difference in the world between teaching a human being and sanding the gears in a machine. The machine does a job. The human being embarks on a quest. The machine hums a dreary, constant drone. The human being sings. One might object that the human being lusts, while the machine cannot. True enough, but the effect of lust, as of all evil habits, is to rob the soul of its freedom. Virtue humanizes and spiritualizes what is part animal in us. Vice brutalizes what is human and spiritual in us. Ultimately it does worse than that. It binds us to a mechanical action. We can see that in the dull gaping stare of a man in the grip of pornography. Scientists, coming round to telling us all what we knew already, say that that vice infantilizes the brain, replacing reason, which infants do not yet possess, with automatism, as of a child sucking contentedly on his pacifier.

We might well ask why the intellectual elite among us—the "cognitive elite" or "knowledge class"—would wish to govern a society of grown men and women crying out for rubber nipples. The quick answer is that our elites themselves have not been well educated, as I have suggested, so that they do not know what harm they do by what Gabriel Marcel has called "techniques of degradation."

There is a more sinister possibility. Just as the owners of large and powerful businesses will accept higher taxes as the price by which they can put their less powerful competitors out of business, so those who have graduated from Harvard and Yale can profit from the degradation of their poorer brethren who may not even have the opportunity to go to college at all. The principal capital that the poor possess is moral. They don't have big bank accounts, they don't own property on the shorefront, and they are not connected with fellow alumni in the boardroom or the halls of government. They have backs and hands and brains, and, if it were not for the itch, they could have the moral force to build solid families and to thrive by their cleanness and courage and self-sacrifice. All you have to do to put them out of the game is to corrupt them. Then you will turn competitors into clients, building for yourself a perpetual underclass. From the profits you gain in corrupting them, managing them, and pretending to champion them in the helplessness you have induced among them, you can ensconce yourself in power and wealth, and live far away from the results of your beneficence. You can do this and hug yourself for it, casting yourself as a lover of single motherhood, "nontraditional families," and other sexual derangements that confuse, impoverish, and vitiate, while accusing your opponents of bigotry and hard-heartedness. Nice work if you can get it.

So, here on our planet Obsessus, the virtue of chastity is not even a faint recollection. It is called abstinence, and it is mocked. Manhood is mocked, although women are praised mainly for impersonating it. The child-making thing is for everything except making children, unless you happen to want children; all is valued according to one's craving. It should go without saying that the Obsessed do not marry very well, and that they are too immature to suppose that their lust might have something to do with their marital failures.

The society that promotes chastity promotes true wedded love. The land of marriage, despite all the troubles that sinful human beings bring upon themselves, is a paradise by comparison with the land of easy fornication and childlessness by choice. In the land of marriage, not on Obsessus, we will find all the glorious expectancy of young people in love; the pilgrimage that begins with an exchange of glances and ends within the temple, with man and woman exchanging vows, before they enter that other temple where they exchange their very bodies; the beauty of a gift given without reserve, at the just time, with due ceremony; and the beauty of the child ever present in their midst; the child who may be born from their loving interchange, and the God eternally young, whom they in their innocence revere.

6

Condoning Everything and Forgiving Nothing

The New Pharisee

The farmer is looking out over his fields, which have begun to sprout seedlings. But his foreman has bad news. "Sir," he says, "I see weeds growing up among the wheat. Your enemy must have scattered them broadside one night when we were not watching."

"No surprise there," the farmer says with a sigh. It is the way of human life, after all. The city is peppered with gossips, petty thieves, mischievous children, knaves, and whores. So it is, so it was, and so will it ever be until the consummation of the world.

"But what shall we do, sir? Do you wish me to go and uproot the weeds now, before they grow?"

The farmer considers for a moment. He could take radical action to bring about some utopian field, or he could live with the weeds. The farmer chooses to live with the weeds. He chooses not to pretend that the world can be made perfect by clever measures or by force.

"No," he says. "If you try to do that, you might root up the good wheat, too. Let them grow up together, and after we have done our reaping, we will separate them out, saving the good and burning the bad."

Readers of the *Washington Post* will likely not have caught my allusion, but that is one of the most fascinating parables of Jesus regarding the Kingdom of God (Matthew 13:24–30). Jesus does not say that the weeds are really good; that we have long had an unreasonable prejudice against weeds; that if we ate the weeds we might find ourselves better off; that a field with a diversity of weeds and wheat is more beautiful than a field of wheat alone. The weeds are bad, but the attempt to eradicate all of them—what the radical aims for—will make matters worse, and much that is good will be destroyed along with the bad.

Thomas Aquinas, considering the parable, pointed out that it is often not suitable to try by statutory law to eliminate every evil. We cannot be hobnailed giants thumping through the fields to pick out little bits of clover among the corn. We should not try to eliminate house fires by pulling down all the houses. We cannot imprison every liar, since no one would be left outside the bars to let us out once we have served our terms.

Because human beings are imperfect—or, as Christians say, because we are sinners, fallen in nature—no society can ever be perfect, and therefore all attempts to make a society perfect must end in complete failure or tyranny. That is due in large part to the fact that, as Shakespeare shows us again and again, there are no rulers or judges who are immune to the moral trouble: "Thieves for their robbery have authority / When judges steal themselves" (*Measure for Measure*).

We are men, for better and for worse. We are not angels; we are not devils. Nor are we machines to be ordered by some perfectly efficient regimen. We will err in judgment, and they who trust themselves the most will be most apt to fall. Instead the just judge, in this the only world we live in, must take into account his own *imperfections*. So says the self-knowing Duke in *Measure for Measure* when he learns that his deputy, Angelo, is set on committing the very crime to which he is condemning to death the brother of the woman he is trying to seduce:

> He who the sword of heaven will bear
> Should be as holy as severe;

Pattern in himself to know,
Grace to stand, and virtue go;
More nor less to others paying
Than by self-offenses weighing.

We have to *tolerate* much, because we ourselves are sinners and give others occasion for tolerance. That is, we have to bear with much that is genuinely bad, because we ourselves are not perfect. "In the course of justice," says Portia to the self-justified Shylock, "none of us should see salvation."

To pretend to perfection is to be a hypocrite. So Jesus says, in the very parable that provided Shakespeare with the title of his play about justice and mercy:

With what judgment ye judge, ye shall be judged; and with what measure ye mete, it shall be measured to you again.

And why beholdest thou the mote that is in thy brother's eye, but considerest not the beam that is in thine own eye?

Or how wilt thou say to thy brother, Let me pull out the mote out of thine eye; and behold, a beam *is* in thine own eye?

Thou hypocrite, first cast out the beam out of thine own eye; and then shalt thou see clearly to cast out the mote out of thy brother's eye. (Matthew 7:2–5)

Jesus is not telling us that it is good to have specks or splinters or planks in our eyes, just as it is not good to have a wheat field laced with weeds. The point is not to let your brother see badly but to acknowledge that you yourself see badly, and maybe worse than your brother sees. We are called to tolerate others because we give those others much to tolerate in ourselves. If we thought first, though, about *not tolerating* what is bad in us, then we might finally see well enough not to pick at the faults of our brothers but to heal them. Tolerance is that important but subordinate virtue by which, instructed in our own weakness, we bear with what is bad without pretending that it is good. We bear with it provisionally, even if sometimes there is nothing we can do about it or ever will be able to do about it. It is something to endure. The Latin root that gives us the word *tolerate* is the same that gives us the Old English *tholian*, to suffer, and the German *dulden*, to be patient.

We are called to tolerate a great deal, but not everything. We are charged with caring for those who are most vulnerable, so Jesus is especially severe with people who harm the bodies or souls of children: "Whoso shall offend one of these little ones which believe in me, it were better for him that a millstone were hanged about his neck, and that he were drowned in the depth of the sea" (Matthew 18:6). Unless he should repent, that is. And that brings us to a further question: if we are to tolerate much, how much must we *forgive*?

The pagan answer might be, "Much less than we will tolerate," because, after all, to forgive is to do something far more difficult than merely to tolerate. But Jesus says otherwise. When Peter asks Him how often he is to forgive his brother—and I do not know whether the amiable Andrew was standing right there when he asked it—he ventured an absurd suggestion. Would it be seven times? Seven, the divine number of the creation itself? Jesus says it should not be seven times but "seventy times seven"—that is, innumerably (Matthew 18:22). We are in fact to forgive *always*, when repentance is offered, for God Himself "maketh His sun to rise on the evil and on the good" (Matthew 5:45), and "if ye forgive not men their trespasses, neither will your Father forgive your trespasses" (Matthew 6:15), and "all have sinned and come short of the glory of God" (Romans 3:23). So says Prospero, in the final words of the last play Shakespeare wrote on his own, in a kind of farewell to the stage. Begging a liberating forgiveness from the audience, their hands to hoist his sails and their cheers to fill them, he reminds them of the Lord's Prayer:

> As you from crimes would pardon'd be,
> Let your indulgence set me free.

We must forgive, because we have been forgiven. There are no exceptions.

But there is still another question to ask. How much must we *condone*? I do not mean put up with. I mean, how much evil should we agree not to call evil? How much evil should we wink at, be complacent about, derive some modest enjoyment from, pat on the head and say it is not so bad after all? And here again the words of Jesus startle. "Be ye therefore perfect, even as your Father who is in heaven is perfect" (Matthew 5:48). That is not a blank perfection, a being free from stain. It is the living perfection of holiness itself. It demands our utmost. So preaches Saint Peter toward the end of his life:

> Gird up the loins of your mind; be sober and hope to the end for the grace that is to be brought unto you at the revelation of Jesus Christ.
>
> As obedient children, do not fashion yourselves according to the former lusts in your ignorance, But as He who hath called you is holy, so be ye holy in all manner of living, because it is written: "Be ye holy; for I am holy." (1 Peter 1:13–16)

We are to condone *no evil*. We do not condone the evil desire even when we do not approve it with evil action, for "whosoever looketh on a woman to lust after her hath committed adultery with her already in his heart" (Matthew 5:28). Bad and good are invited together to the wedding feast, but the complacent man who arrives dressed just as he is, in contempt of the holiness of the feast, hears the question, "Friend, how camest thou in hither not having a wedding garment?" (Matthew 22:12). And he has nothing to say. The thief who pleaded for Christ's forgiveness from the Cross heard that he would be with Him that day in Paradise, but this nonchalant man, blank, not repenting, not perhaps even aware of a need to repent, is cast out into the darkness.

To sum it up: as regards evil, we are to *tolerate much, forgive all, and condone nothing.*

It is liberating to do so. It sets one free from the bondage of self-righteousness, that most insidious evil. It also sets others free from the burden of evil, because they will be discouraged from engaging it and given instead opportunity to leave the evil behind, when the rejoicing will be great in heaven for the lost sheep that is found. Forgiveness—not condoning, or even toleration—is what makes the feast possible for the dissolute son who has come home.

But Life Under Compulsion is a different matter altogether. By the dictates of Life Under Compulsion, we are to *condone much, tolerate little, and forgive nothing.* This requires some explanation.

Freedom and Virtue

Which pagan philosopher or Christian father believed that liberty without virtue was a chimera? That is a trick question. *They all believed it.* Even the Epicureans believed it. Here is the Epicurean philosopher and poet Lucretius describing what most people give their lives to:

> How sweet, to watch from the shore the wind-whipped ocean
> Toss someone else's ship in a mighty struggle;
> Not that the man's distress is cause for mirth—
> Your freedom from those troubles is what's sweet;
> And sweet, to see great lines of soldiers marshaled
> In the plains of war, when you are free from peril;
> But nothing is sweeter than to dwell in the calm
> Temples of truth, the strongholds of the wise.
> You can, from there, look down upon others wandering
> Randomly, straying, seeking the path of life,
> Warring with all their talent, wrestling for rank,
> Night and day straining with the utmost toil
> To fight their way to the heights of wealth and power.
> O heart of man, how pitiful and blind!

Lucretius is describing, with something quite different from Christian mercy, the vice-feeding pursuit of power, position, and wealth. We might call it covetousness or ambitious pride. In other passages of his work he will similarly shed a tear or two, and break out into loud laughter, at the sight of people ruining their lives with lust. The ruin comes not simply as a consequence. All vice rots us from within, riddling us with termites in the very act, regardless of whether our wealth will prop us up for a while before complete collapse.

But there's more. Lucretius sees that there is something *compulsive* about vice. The man standing atop the promontory, looking down upon the merchant's ship toiling in the waves, or the general's army swarming in the plain, is *free*. Granted, the vision of freedom is still too limited, too much a reaction against what is bad rather than a generous and vital love of what is good. But what the poet does see, he sees clearly. If you have disciplined yourself *against* the common vices, you will be like that wise man on the mountain. Other people are caught in the frenzy. You are not.

The sense here is that good habits and bad habits differ not only in their objects but also in the way we experience them. The good habit or virtue is what Aristotle called a "second nature." It is a power; it feels right and ordinary to us and makes it easy for us to do good things. An artist who works hard at his craft will eventually be able to draw with just a few easy strokes the gentle fall of a girl's hair; he doesn't have to break out a slide rule. The brave soldier hears the bullets whistling about and he experiences a perfectly natural fear, but he also experiences the liberating habit of courage, and he collects himself and determines what to do, not to rush the enemy in the heedless despair that merely looks like courage, and not to run off in terror. What would be impossible for a coward is possible for him. A man who possesses the power of temperance attends the wedding and has a couple of drinks of wine that gladdens the heart. He does not have to drink the wine, but he does not have to abstain from it either. It is an innocent thing to do in the circumstances, and it adds the flush of merriment to the festive occasion. He does not embarrass himself in drunkenness. He does not *have to drink.*

The vices are not like that. The vices do not give us power over our impulses from within or over objects of fear, wrath, or desire that meet us from without. The vices give those impulses and objects power over us. The gambler sits at the keno machine, draining down his credit card as he presses the button for a new game, time after time after time. The student sits at his book and his mind begins to wander, and he feels he cannot help himself, he *must turn* to his favorite mode of distraction. He spins his wheels in sloth. He knows, when he is in the slough, that there's nothing for it but to get out of the car and walk. But he cannot do it. He has begun to "like" the sound of the spinning wheels and the spurting of the mud up to the windows. He has begun to "enjoy" the feeling of powerlessness. He courts it.

In *The Faerie Queene,* Edmund Spenser gives us a parade of the seven capital vices, each one associated with its appropriate compulsions and debilities. Here is a fine example:

> And him besides rides fierce revenging Wrath
> Upon a lion, loath for to be led;
> And in his hand a burning brand he hath,
> The which he brandisheth about his head;
> His eyes did hurl forth sparkles fiery red,
> And stared stern on all that him beheld,
> As ashes pale of hue and seeming dead;
> And on his dagger still his hand he held,
> Trembling through hasty rage, when choler in him swelled.
>
> His ruffian raiment all was stained with blood
> Which he had spilt, and all to rags yrent,
> Through unadvised rashness woxen wood;
> For of his hands he had no government,
> Nor cared for blood in his avengement:
> But when the furious fit was overpast

His cruel facts he often would repent;
Yet, wilful man, he never would forecast
How many mischiefs should ensue his heedless haste.

Full many mischiefs follow cruel Wrath:
Abhorred Bloodshed and tumultuous Strife,
Unmanly Murder, and unthrifty Scathe,
Bitter Despite, with Rancor's rusty knife,
And fretting Grief the enemy of life;
All these, and many evils more haunt Ire,
The swelling Spleen, and Frenzy raging rife,
The shaking Palsy, and Saint Francis' Fire:
Such one was Wrath, the last of this ungodly tire.

What looks like power is actually frailty. Wrath rides upon a lion and waves a flaming sword roundabout. But he cannot control himself. He trembles with rage—and shakes with palsy. His sword burns—and he is ravaged within by Saint Francis's fire, the inflammatory disease erysipelas. He has no foresight, only hindsight, and in that hindsight he often regrets his evil deeds, too late. He is an agent of disintegration, bringing strife and bloodshed wherever he goes. "I burn, I burn, I burn!" will cry a later figure in the poem, an emblem of this very vice, leaping into the water that cannot quench the fire.

Dante, too, understood that there is a mad self-compulsion in evil, a reduction of man to a helpless caricature. The avaricious souls in Hell roll a giant boulder against their indistinguishable "enemies" the prodigals, as they shout, "Why do you fritter?" and the prodigals respond, "Why the fists so tight?" And they do this over and over, for all eternity. The lustful are whipped about in a whirlwind just as they allowed their sexual passions to hurl them here, there, everywhere on earth. They cannot stop. The bribe-taking politicians, they of the sticky fingers, spend eternity trying to escape the pool of boiling tar into which they are plunged, tricking the harpoon-wielding demons who are supposed to keep them in that pool; it is petty graft and slapstick constabulary, world without end. Satan at the bottom of Hell, fixed to his waist in ice, flaps his wings incessantly, raising the wind that freezes the River Cocytus and imprisons him there. He cannot cease; he will not cease. He has what Milton's Satan will boast of, a "fixed mind." They are *determined* in their evil: fixed in the cramped little cage of sin. Or, as Lucretius says, describing the frenetic and frustrated activity of a man who is always wanting more, who flees from city to country villa and back to the city again: "We flee ourselves, whom we can never flee."

To give yourself over to an evil is, in some measure, to pretend that what you know is wrong is right, and then, to justify yourself, you must give yourself over to it all the more. The drunk continues to drink, in part to help him forget that he is a drunk. The man addicted to pornography knows that it is gross, and in his self-loathing he turns back to the pornography. To go far in vice is to force an inversion in values. You know that you are weak, but you must persuade yourself that the weakness is strength. You welcome the compulsion. Rather than admit that you *can free yourself of the evil*, an admission that must come with great pain, you declare that the evil is good and pitch yourself into it headfirst. It becomes your master. Your will is formally free: no one is compelling you to do the evil you do. But it is existentially in prison. As Jesus says: "He who sins is a slave to sin" (John 8:34).

In other words, the moral law is not the enemy of human liberty. It is its condition. Animals act by necessity, but as Pope Leo XIII puts it in *Libertas praestantissimum*, his encyclical on human liberty, "he who is free can either act or not act, can do this or do that, as he pleases, because his judgment precedes his choice." The ordination of reason in these choices is called *law*: "a fixed rule of teaching what is to be done and what is to be left undone." Without law, "the freedom of our will would be our ruin," and "nothing more foolish can be uttered or conceived than the notion that, because man is free by nature, he is therefore exempt from law. Were this the case, it would follow that to become free we must be deprived of reason; whereas the truth is that we are bound to submit to law precisely because we are free by our very nature."

This insight is the common patrimony of the Greek and Roman philosophers and poets, the Hebrew prophets, the Gospels and the Christian fathers. It used to be quite uncontroversial. When Maria von Trapp, the heroine of the story that became *The Sound of Music*, was asked why she maintained such strong discipline in her new home in America, she replied that she wanted to set her children free from being mastered by their passions. The only remarkable thing about that statement was that anyone should have found it remarkable.

A New Kind of Pharisee

"All this talk is beside the point," says the sophomore, with a toss of the head. "We are not supposed to judge, you know." The argument has all the force of a child sticking out his tongue.

The fact is we *must* judge. We are moral beings. We think; we judge this to be good and that to be bad; we judge that this is a permissible way to attain the good and that is not; we judge that this good here must be subordinated to that more exalted good there. We can no more cease to judge than we can cease to think.

What we must not do, if we heed the Sermon on the Mount, is to judge others according to standards more severe than those by which we judge ourselves, or to pretend that we know about the state of someone else's soul when we hardly know the state of our own, or to judge according to trivialities, such as whether the poor man tithes his mint and cumin, weeds that sprout up at the side of his hovel, and not according to the clean heart that God desires. The same Jesus who warns us against superficial, hasty, merciless, or hypocritical judgments condones *no evil at all* and judges a whole host of our favorite sins by comparing them to the filth that comes out of us after a big meal:

Do ye not perceive, that whatsoever thing from without entereth into the man, it cannot defile him;

Because it entereth not into his heart, but into the belly, and goeth out into the draught, purging all meats?

That which cometh out of the man, that defileth the man.

For from within, out of the heart of men, proceed evil thoughts, adulteries, fornications, murders,

Thefts, covetousness, wickedness, deceit, lasciviousness, an evil eye, blasphemy, pride, foolishness:

All these evil things come from within, and defile the man. (Mark 7:18–23)

The old Pharisee thought he was better than other men because he fulfilled the externals of the law. He did not have true virtue. It was something he wore, like a robe, but it was not the light of his heart shining from within. In Jesus's parable, that self-satisfied man goes to the Temple to praise himself, not God. He doesn't take other men's wives, he doesn't shill for the Romans, he fasts twice a week, he coaches Little League and gives to the United Way.

Meanwhile, the publican—a Jewish trusty for the Romans, one who collected their taxes and kept for himself everything he could rummage up beyond their take—stood in the back and "would not lift up so much as his eyes unto heaven, but smote upon his breast, saying, God be merciful to me a sinner" (Luke 18:13). Jesus does not say that it is bad to fast and good to fleece your countrymen. *He assumes that we will judge the deeds rightly.* The men are another matter; God sees into the heart.

Now there is a way we can be a New Pharisee while standing in the publican's position. It's to say, "I don't go to church, because the church is full of hypocrites." One more won't do any harm, then! Or to say, "I am not prissy, like my friend Amy here, who *really wants* to do what I do but doesn't have the courage." Or to say, "I am glad I'm free and easy with the so-called moral rules, because all I see from the other side are glum faces and frustration." Dietrich von Hildebrand called this sort of reversal "sin mysticism," as if there were something really impressive and interesting about being wicked, and said that the New Pharisee stood in the back of the church or outside of it altogether, saying, "God, I thank thee, that I am a sinner and a publican, and not like this self-righteous churchgoer here!" It has become downright trite, this reversal of "good" and "bad," much to the comfort of people who don't want the trouble it takes to acquire a real virtue.

But there is a New and Improved Pharisee, flabby in moral action and as stern as steel in judgment *against others*, not for their actions but for their assertions or demurrals. In other words, the New Pharisee, in bondage to one favorite sin or another, *demands judgment in favor of the sin*. In the new dispensation, we are justified not by what we do but by our *thinking and saying the approved thing about what other people do*, particularly if that approved thing is itself wrong. We are *compelled to condone*. The boy and girl are shacking up? Better that than some impossible pursuit of chastity. Have they begotten a child? Let's throw a party! But they are going to exterminate it. Well, let's make sure we give them a sympathy card. The politician told a pack of lies? But that politician is *good*, because he has made *these assertions*, which are approved. *Correct thinking* covers a multitude of sins. Condone, or else.

"I thank you, Lord," says the New and Improved Pharisee, "that you have made me so tolerant," by which he means that he condones evil, or that he is indifferent to it or insensible of it, or that he even cultivates it. In any case, it proves no burden to him. "I love being tolerant, not like those intolerant people there," and yet, almost before he finishes the sentence, he pitches himself into further and more absurd judgment against his neighbor.

For the moral faculty cannot remain idle. *Some object* must take the place of genuine good. So we witness a most strange phenomenon, which the New and Improved Pharisee embodies. The NIP is a ferocious judge, according to an alternate moral "law," which he adopts with a fury and enforces without mercy, since he must keep down the nagging awareness that this alternate law is phony. On Monday he says that God really prefers him to the churchgoer. On Tuesday he says that there is no God. On Wednesday he plays god, and is all the more severe in proportion as his "law" is trivial. We are talking here about an inverted etiquette raised to the status of inexorable moral rule. And because its enforcers are aware of no sin—conveniently defining what is wrong as what other people believe—their ambition is unbounded.

The terrible irony should not be lost on us. The state where I live, Rhode Island, was founded by a Baptist minister, Roger Williams, who wished to establish a colony characterized by freedom of worship, at least for his fellow Protestants. Whatever one may think should be the relations between churches and the state, one cannot fail to be stirred by the noble words inscribed in Latin on the frieze of the capitol's rotunda: RARA FELICITAS TEMPORUM UBI SENTIRE QUAE VELIS ET QUAE SENTIAS DICERE LICET—*The rare happiness of times when one may think what one will and speak what one thinks.* Now, when the name of Christ is treated as an obscenity that may not be uttered within the walls of a public school, we dare not express what we think about any number of things, if we do not want to be dragged before the commissars of correct thinking and signed over for reeducation. The common engine of such reeducation, the mildest form of punishment for thoughtcrime, is "sensitivity training." Bullies do not always lose their sense of humor. More severe punishments include loss of employment and public campaigns to destroy your reputation.

The New and Improved Law

I have sometimes wished that the thought police would get around to issuing a handy list of things to which we are supposed to give our vocal assent. It is hard to smother your common sense, to ignore history and the evidence of your eyes, and to turn reason into intellectual pretzels. All that requires a good deal of self-suppression. The task would be made a little easier if we could be informed beforehand what to think. We are plebeians, after all, and can't be expected to perform the mental gymnastics of our patrician masters. But since they have not come up with such a list, and since, if the truth be known, they themselves are often reduced to catching up with the latest rectitudes, I have decided to provide one here below.

Thou shalt not call an unmarried woman "Miss." Thou shalt not feed thy children cupcakes. Thou shalt not think that women should not be soldiers. Thou shalt recycle thy bottles.

Thou shalt not speak about God in a public school. Thou shalt not say that the Ten Commandments are commandments. Thou shalt not speak ill of any culture, with the following exceptions: American, British, medieval, Christian, and Catholic. Thou shalt not speak well of those. Thou shalt not laugh at certain jokes. Thou shalt not vote for a conservative, if thou canst find one.

Thou shalt not say that a man is biologically incapable of marrying another man. Thou shalt not decline to march in the following parades. Thou shalt not agree to march in the following parades. Thou shalt not have anything good to say about popes and priests. Thou shalt not say what you believe unless it is approved by pundits on television.

Thou shalt not say that contemporary music is ugly and banal. Thou shalt not shop in the following places. Thou shalt purchase the following product, on pain of targeting by the Internal Revenue Service. Thou shalt attend these sex education classes. Thou shalt not utter a word of complaint about them.

Thou shalt not exhibit any fondness for the American South. Thou shalt adore Abraham Lincoln and abhor Robert E. Lee. Thou shalt not say that women have not been persecuted from of old. Thou shalt not say that men are for women and women are for men.

Thou shalt not give thy son a toy pistol. Thou shalt not shoot a rubber band at the back of thy schoolmate's head. Thou shalt not say "bang." Thou shalt not complain when a boy claims to be a girl and uses thy shower. Thou shalt celebrate what we like, whether it liketh thee or not.

Thou shalt not dress thy older daughter in a dress. Thou shalt not say, "My nation are heathen fools." Thou shalt not wear a cross around thy neck in a hospital. Thou shalt not pray too close to someone going to slay her child. Thou shalt not spank thy smart-mouth. Thou shalt not sleep thy children more than one to a room. Thou shalt not look askance at the fornicator. Thou shalt lend other people's money to people whose prospects for repayment are not good. Thou shalt allocate other people's money to thy clients.

Thou shalt not disagree with a social worker. Thou shalt not speak up at an open meeting, unless thou art called upon, and unless thou sayest what those who hold the meeting want to hear. Thou shalt not disagree with a policeman. Thou shalt not bring toothpaste on an airplane.

Thou shalt not say disparaging things about global warming. Thou shalt not collect rainwater in thy cistern. Thou shalt not kill the weasel that is eating thine eggs. Thou shalt read the poetry of Maya Angelou, and thou shalt pretend to be impressed by it. Thou shalt admire soccer. Thou shalt sneer at everything more than three minutes old. Thou shalt pursue orgasms. Thou shalt not deny the harlot her due. Thou shalt be feminist in thought, word, and deed.

Thou shalt, O child, learn in school what opinions thou must have. It needs not that thou should learn grammar, history, poetry, geography, the natural sciences, or mathematics. It needs not that thou read the great authors of the Western heritage. School is not for those. It is for the building up of the New and Improved Pharisee, to torment his parents withal in the evening, if they should yet retain something of the liberty of common sense and ordinary virtue.

Thou shalt, thou shalt not, on and on, with no end in sight. None of it really unites us as a people; none of it has the power to make us good. He who sins is a slave to sin. We have become the slaves of slaves.

7

No History but the Inevitable

The Minotaur

In 1940, when the Nazis attacked their supposed racial kinfolk in Norway and set up a puppet government under the odious Quisling, Sigrid Undset fled with her son Hans to the countryside at Lillehammer and then across the mountains into Sweden. She and Hans spent a short time hiding there from the Lords of the World, then procured airline tickets to Moscow, the capital city of the Other Lords of the World. After two weeks of communist penury and drabness—long lines of people waiting for miserable cuts of meat in a butcher's; empty shops; people walking, walking, walking along the streets seemingly without aim—they rode a train, without running water in their bathroom, across the continent to Vladivostok, then left that sewage-ridden hole for imperialist Japan and Lords of the East, and finally to the United States and freedom. She wrote about what she saw and what she thought in a remarkable book, *Return to the Future*, published in 1942, when it was by no means certain that all of Europe would not finally be reduced to the stupidity of Hitlerism or Stalinism. Germany, Russia, and Japan: all places where life was lived under the severe compulsion of the state, allowing for differences in culture (Undset saw much to admire in Japan).

She chose her title advisedly, and with her usual biting irony. The continents of Europe and Asia were crawling with people who were sure, absolutely sure, that they were to spearhead the next Great Leap Forward in human evolution. The master races would dominate, because they *must*: their superior intellects would assert themselves, as surely as an amoeba engulfs its prey or a lawyer seizes his fee, as inevitably as grandchildren are smarter and more able than their grandparents, as reliably as Roman Empires rise and rise and never decline—for it never happens that whole civilizations commit suicide, or rot from within, or sag of their own dead weight, or are swept off the earth by Huns.

Indeed, the assumption of inevitability relieves the Lords of the World from justifying their wicked or stupid deeds. No one argues against the law of gravity. It simply is. To oppose "progress," let us say by asking about the destination to which we are progressing, is to be an irritant, a wrench in the gears of the rumbling and unstoppable juggernaut leveling every stubborn thing in its way. To say, instead, "I should not like to have my village destroyed by the innovation," to honor the past in piety and gratitude, is regarded as simply evil. No argument is really ever made against the pious man. He is sneered at. He is dusty and old. He cannot—here comes the cliché—"think outside the box." He is afraid of *change*, even if all he asks is what is to be changed and why. He is "medieval." It never occurs to the Lords of the World to consider the dynamism of the real Middle Ages. It never occurs to anyone who has spent more than an hour gracing the Lords with attention that the Middle Ages were a time of liberties—of chartered guilds, schools, and towns, from the Atlantic to the shores of the Don.

For Undset, the future of Europe could be found only by a *return*—that is, a recovery of the free associations of people that had characterized the Middle Ages generally, and Norway and Iceland in particular. Anyone who has read her novels set in that era—*Kristin Lavransdatter* and *The Master of Hestviken*—or her biographies of Catherine of Siena or Angela Merici knows that she is a meticulous and honest historian. She does not dabble in sentiment. She knows how bloody the fractious cities of northern Italy were. She knows that the Christianity brought to Norway by Saint Olaf was still half pagan. But the medieval kings and dukes had not the technology, even if they had had the desire, to place vast stretches of country under their direct and meddlesome control. For the most part, affairs were determined locally. Therefore there were, in reality, thousands of small "republics," whether or not they showed up on a map. Indeed, the *res* in the Latin *res publica* has just the same meaning as the Icelandic *thing* and the Norwegian *ting*: the *public thing*, the gathering of free men in the pursuit of the common good.

These *things* were necessary, she suggests, because of the nature of the land whence the men had to wrest a living: Norway, with its narrow strip of arable land, hemmed between mountains and bogs to the east and rocky fjords to the west, and with its beautiful and sun-filled summer, heartbreakingly short as it was. The heroes of Norwegian culture were not, as in Germany, men like Hagen of the *Nibelungenlied*, whose loyalty to his lord trumps the moral law and common decency. They were rescuers, men who risked or gave their lives upon the open sea to help their fellows in a shipwreck, or who tramped across miles of snow to save men trapped in a storm, or at least to bring back their bodies.

People in Undset's day were already saying that Germany had been taken over by a tiny self-made military elite and that the Germans were victims just as the people the Nazis subjugated were. Sigrid Undset wasn't buying. She and her neighbors remembered having housed and fed German children after the first war, and some of those same children they recognized as grown men, trying to destroy the land that showed them mercy. Instead she said that there must have been something abnormal about a people—she was thinking mainly of northern Germans and the Prussians—who seemed to admire the absolutist. She was drawing a connection between the commission of unnatural crimes and Life Under Compulsion. We might say she saw that people who believed that their ways were *inevitable* would go out of their way to make damned sure that everyone else helped make them so.

People who do not study history, said George Santayana, are doomed to repeat it. I have come to detest that dictum. We will be doomed perhaps to repeat its follies; those are easy enough. We will not be blessed to repeat its triumphs; those are not easy. They are certainly not inevitable. One thing that history teaches us abundantly is that, although human nature does not change, human events are unpredictable. Saint Jerome expressed the astonishment of the citizens of the Roman Empire when, in 410, the Visigoth warlord Alaric put Rome to the torch. "The world sinks into ruin," wrote Saint Jerome. "Yes! But shameful to say our sins still live and flourish. The renowned city, the capital of the Roman Empire, is swallowed up in one tremendous fire; and there is no part of the earth where Romans are not in exile." It had been seven centuries since an invader had taken the city. Even the brilliant Hannibal never managed to do it.

Now, if we learn from history that our achievements are not secured forever, and that cultural progress, however one wishes to define it, is by no means uniform or dependable, then we will not be so sure about the next wonder with which our controllers wish to bless us. And that robs the controllers of their favorite tool. Consider, after all, the strategic situation of those who wish to promote the unnatural, whatever it may happen to be—bloody in Hitler, obscene in Hugh Hefner. How do you get people en masse to submit to madness? By compulsion.

The Future Cometh, Whether We Like It or Not

Systems of compulsion breed the unnatural, just as the unnatural requires systems of compulsion to confirm it. Consider communism, a system so insane that it could survive only by compulsion—through show trials and executions and the gulag.

We must not think that these acts of compulsion were merely imposed upon a defenseless people, from without. They rose also from within. In a chapter of *The Gulag Archipelago* bitterly entitled

"The History of Our Sewage Disposal System," Aleksandr Solzhenitsyn enumerates the lies, the treacheries, and the abominations of Article 58 of the Soviet criminal code, that which sent so many millions of articles of human sewage to the miserable labor camps or to their graves. "Section 12," he writes, "concerned itself closely with the conscience of our citizens: it dealt with the *failure to make a denunciation* of any action of the types listed. And the penalty for the mortal sin of failure to make a denunciation *carried no maximum limit!*" (emphasis in the original). A great wave of wives in 1940 were arrested for failure to denounce their husbands. Nobody noticed. Subverting and weakening the government, says Solzhenitsyn, "could include any idea which did not coincide with or rise to the level of intensity of the ideas expressed in the newspaper on any particular day." That was no exaggeration. Solzhenitsyn cites the cheerleading Soviet poet Mayakovsky:

And he who sings not with us today
    is against
        us!

That meant those who were insufficiently enthusiastic for the revolution—insufficiently infected with the compulsion. As early as 1919, says Solzhenitsyn, the Soviets were devouring their own (just as, we might note, the "progressive" of Wednesday who calls for the latest innovation in debauchery—say, marriage à trois—will devour the "progressive" of Tuesday who happily waved the flag of Sodom). Was it not time to thin out the ranks of the intelligentsia? "Once again Mayakovsky came to the rescue":

Think
    about the Komsomol
        for days and for weeks!
Look over
    your ranks,
        watch them with care.

Are all of them
   really
      Komsomols?
Or are they
   only
      pretending to be?

Mayakovsky, the great compulsive futurist, shot himself in 1930, disillusioned by the supposed "philistinism" of his motherland under Stalin. He could not wait for what he thought was inevitable.

The survival of communism had to be ensured by the compulsions from without. But survival is not life. Communism could only *live* as a fire in the hearts of its adherents if it promised something in return: not heaven but the great communist Future, the Peaceable Dictatorship of the Proletariat, the consummation of history.

I have suggested a connection between compulsion and the unnatural. Those connections were everywhere to be found in Soviet Russia. It is natural for people to worship God. The Soviets were relentlessly atheistic. It is natural for people to love their homesteads, where their mothers and fathers were laid to rest. The Soviets turned those homesteads into collectives. It is natural for children to turn to their parents for instruction and to be loyal to them. The Soviets raised schoolchildren to watch their parents with a wary eye. It is natural for people to welcome home their prisoners of war. The Soviets accused them of treason and sent them to their deaths. Some historians, moderate tea-sipping apologists for the bloody Lenin, if not for the bloody Stalin, will say that the Soviets had good ideas at the beginning but betrayed them or went overboard. Not so. The ideas were deranged from the beginning, and bred derangement. "Sin will pluck on sin," says Shakespeare. Drink from the flagon of the unnatural, and you must drink more and more, or worse and worse, to "justify" the first, or to perpetuate its evil thrill. Again: virtue is a habit consonant with nature. Vice is a compulsion.

What does all this have to do with us, and with how we teach our youth? Communism outside of China and a few straggling places may be moribund, but the compulsion is not. The compulsion has simply changed its object. No one takes Marx's economics terribly seriously. But maybe the real Future is the Peaceable Haven of Hedonism, with more genders than there are flavors of ice cream. Maybe the real Future is the Rational Rabbit Warren, wherein most of mankind, brainless bunnies, have their lives managed for them by graduates of Harvard and Yale. Maybe it is the Desert of Dead Men, a depopulated world, to give more room for nightshade and lizards. Maybe it is the Feminist Fairy Tale, wherein women rule things in androgynous harmony, and men, magically reduced in size, strength, and aggressiveness, actually go along with it instead of checking out and making things miserable for everyone. These things must be! History dictates it! Do not fall on the wrong side of History! *Der Zukunft kommt schon! Mach schnell!*

The dominion of the Soviets in large part rested upon their capacity to induce fear, not only in others but also in themselves. The fear was not simply about losing material things. Nor was it the altogether healthy awe before the holy God, and a fear to do evil. It was a generalized fear of being judged by "history," something utterly undefined, constantly shifting, impersonal, deaf to appeal, and unforgiving. They were like people walking over loose boards set haphazardly over a great field of quicksand, with no end in sight.

We are like that, too. One false step, one "incorrect" utterance, one check sent to the "wrong" organization, one roll of the eyes, and unless we hasten to abase ourselves publicly and apologize for having enjoyed a rare moment of freedom and health, we sink in the quicksand, and no one will dare to throw us a rope.

So we submit, within and without, to the domination. But the desire to dominate is antithetical to the generosity of love. "The Son of Man," says Jesus, "came not to be served but to serve." The arrow is pointed in both directions: the *libido dominandi* makes common cause with the *dominium libidinis*, the dominion of lust. Love sets the lover free; indeed, without freedom there can be no love. Lust, whether for a human body or for a body politic, laced with the tang of evil, is addictive precisely because it is wrong. The Soviet officers in the camps knew that tang, which first repels but soon *compels.* The outlines of that hideous strength are coming into view—a vast system of compulsion, feeding and fed by revulsion against the sweetness of such natural goods as the family and the innocence of children; compulsion that masks state domination as democracy and commercial manipulation as the satisfaction of desires. Call it the Compulsion Archipelago.

And What Has Happened to History?

As I have suggested, people who really study history know that the ages are littered with the wreckage of "inevitable" things. That is why, in Life Under Compulsion, you may study history only as *inevitable progress toward where you are now and, beyond you, to the object that compels.* You may not honor it in its own right. You must also surround yourself with new and improved "technology," lest your mind begin to wander toward those ages past. Psychological techniques of degradation must merge with the technological.

And of course, the computer, the "screen," now surrounds us. One may, no doubt, use the computer to find historical needles in contemporary haystacks. I use it as a Bible concordance and as a quick—and not wholly reliable—tracker of etymologies. But the computer, like the television (and like the television now more than ever), blares forth the present and buries the past. The wise and morose Preacher warns us that there is nothing new under the sun; the screen fairly shouts that there are only new things under the sun, new and improved, new and bold, new and challenging, new and progressive.

The computer on the desk of the student in school knows no history. It is not like a book, worn at the edges by human hands. No little child has written a note in it, long ago. It will not be passed down to the children of the children who use it. Its "meaning" is that there is no enduring meaning. The book invites us into a conversation with another human being. The computer, as a machine, is not like that, although we may *use* it as a telephone or telegraph, just as the glass and steel skyscraper, as a building that dwarfs the human and reduces him to dust, may still be used for conversations and assignations. What the child learns from the machine is the superiority of the machine, and the relentless and supposedly inevitable triumph of the machine. And the machine runs on, deafening us with noise and news.

The only way we can endure all this noise, all this news, very little of which is actually new at all, is to give up comparing one day's false novelty against the false novelty of the day before. We surrender. What did the president say today? What will the House Speaker reply? Who caught the latest no-talent singer on the beach with the latest no-talent starlet? Did you see the trailer for the new *Star Wars* movie? Where can I buy that new flea powder?

Now you may understand the demonic urge to replace history and geography with social studies and current events.

When we study history in earnest, not reducing it to our current preoccupations—not, for instance, making Jefferson into a tyrant because he owned slaves and Elizabeth Stanton into a heroine because she was a feminist—we climb a mountaintop, from whose vantage the human story may be seen in all its glory and its shame. It is a liberating experience. Machiavelli once wrote to a friend describing his daily life in exile from the Florentine court. He'd wander over to the local watering hole, drinking and playing dice with the ruffians all day, but when he came back home he would change his clothes, don a clean tunic, and open his treasured works of Livy. He was communing with the ancients.

We see, atop that mountain, the variegated and undetermined course of human history. It is like the slow and gradual transformation of a landscape, of hills and woodlands, streams and grassy fields. In general, over the long term, we see improvements in technology and periods of genuine cultural flourishing. But we also see periods when nothing much happens, or when the human things are given over to neglect and decay. That tangle of ivy and bramble covers what used to be a barn. In that field there used to be a school. The books the children learned from have returned to the dust.

We are not compelled by some overarching Law of History. What if the corrupt and avaricious Carthaginian senate had granted Hannibal the supplies he needed? What if the Athenians had not built their navy at the urging of Themistocles? What if Alexander had been felled by a stray arrow in his battle against the Persian emperor Darius? What if, the night before his final statement at the Diet of Worms, Martin Luther had submitted to the authority of the Church? What if the eastern traders had never made it to China and never found what we now know as gunpowder? What if the devilish Hitler had not turned against the devilish Stalin?

We cannot know what would have happened.

When we survey human history, we experience also the wonder of the ancient, the immemorial. We look at a tombstone in a Roman cemetery and read the inscription, *sponsa optima*, the best of wives, and we feel the pull of kinship across the centuries. We look at the Arch of Titus and see, celebrated on its massive pillars, the destruction of Jerusalem and the raiding of the Temple, and we feel the prickle of astonishment, for those same Jews have returned, the Roman Empire is long gone, and still there are men who would happily sweep them into the sea. We enter the great library of John Adams, and it feels like a chapel—it is meant to feel like a chapel—and we handle the books that he handled and see his history in the light of the history that he read, from which he learned so much about the persistence of human folly and ambition, and the tenuousness of liberty.

The study of the past is also, often, an exercise in humility. While the smug are nervously trammeled up in their self-opinion, the humble are free to rejoice in what is genuinely great or noble or beautiful. The adulator of the new *must* believe that a great oblong in brick and glass and steel marks an "advance" in every respect from Chartres or Notre Dame de Paris, but the humble student of history has no stake in that game. He is free to wonder at the glory that a supposedly benighted people could accomplish, and then free to wonder where the real artistic darkness is to be found, then or now. The adulator of the new *must* believe that the free-verse skitterings of the hottest political poet are more worthy of attention and love than are the timeless lyrics of Wordsworth—that a poem that scratches the pustules of race and creed and sex and more sex is "relevant," while Wordsworth's "Michael," a blank-verse narrative about an old shepherd and his beloved son who strayed into dissipation, can mean nothing to a boy growing up fatherless in one of our cities, and ought therefore to be ignored.

History, by its very ambiguity, sets our judgment free. The crisis of the instant (and everything of the instant, we know, is a crisis; there is a financial crisis, an educational crisis, an international crisis, a religious crisis; the baby is crying, the dog has messed on the floor, one nation has bombed another, the wife has gained twenty pounds) demands an immediate and decisive scratch. History, not so.

Was Woodrow Wilson a good president? Was he even a good man? He detested the privilege of the rich at Princeton and broke the grip of the fraternities. He instituted discussion periods for every course in the humanities to temper lectures with human conversation. He believed that the black race was inferior to the white race and accepted the fact on "modern" and "scientific" grounds. He resegregated those parts of the federal workforce that had been integrated. He believed so strongly in securing international peace through his League of Nations that he sowed the seeds of World War II to win approval for it. He allowed abstractions like "self-determination" to blind him to human loyalties and to the long and rich histories of what had been self-governing provinces of the now-destroyed empire of Austria-Hungary. He was a "progressive" who admired the writings of the conservative Edmund Burke. He might have been defeated for reelection in 1916 were it not for several thousand votes in California. He might never have won election in the first place in 1912 were it not for the boundless ambition of Teddy Roosevelt. He was a stern moralist who never doubted the correctness of his convictions. He possessed both the strengths and the shortcomings of the scholar. He was greater than Clemenceau and Lloyd George, yet they played him for a fool.

Nothing like that broad view of things is possible when one is down in the mire. But what about the teacher in the mire?

Let me assert a general rule. Education is liable to corruption to the extent that it turns away from fields in which reliable knowledge and expertise are necessary toward those in which the teacher may indulge his opinions and predilections.

The study of medieval literature, for example, is less liable to corruption than is the study of contemporary poetry, for the plain reason that the former actually requires a great deal of hard-won expertise, in medieval language, in poetic forms now foreign to us, in medieval history and culture, and in some rather sophisticated habits of reading. If you are going to do an honest job in high school teaching Chaucer's *Canterbury Tales*, you have to know some Middle English, you have to know something of Chaucer's predecessors Dante and Boccaccio, you have to know about the liturgical seasons of Lent and Eastertide, you have to know who Thomas Becket was and why that's important, you have to know what a pilgrimage was, you have to be alert to Chaucer's irony and to how medieval artists wove motifs subtly and not-so-subtly throughout the whole of a vast work—you have to know and appreciate quite a few things, and that means that both you and the students will be checking your contemporary itches at the door. In short, it's good to study Chaucer because he will not only provide you with an unexpected view of the current unpleasantness but also give you a chance to set that unpleasantness aside for a while.

You leave the same old same old news, and you pick up what is truly new to you because it is so old. The new is dead on arrival; the old is rich and strange. You experience that richness and strangeness in the company of a teacher who does the same; current events fade for a while into their well-deserved insignificance; and the experience of beauty does what partisan politics can never do, uniting the soul of the teacher and the soul of the student in the love of something beyond their capacity to bring into being, but not beyond their capacity to admire.

The Beast in the Maze

When we lose the sense of transcendence, when in our hearts and minds the things of time are no longer oriented toward eternity, then, writes Jacques Maritain in *The Range of Reason*, it is not only that "Truth and Justice, good and evil, faithfulness, all the standards of conscience, henceforth perfectly relativized, become radically contingent." That would be disastrous enough. Man might then eat, drink, and be sardonically miserable, dying on the morrow, and never soon enough.

But man is not made for epicurean apathy. He is made to find himself by giving of himself wholly. When Jesus says, "Whosoever will save his life shall lose it," He is expressing a law of Being itself. *Bonum diffusivum sui*, say the schoolmen: the Good ever seeks to pour itself forth, and if man cannot submit himself and all his works to God, then he will lose himself instead in the immanent. "The absolute or positive atheist," says Maritain, "hands himself over, body and soul, to the ever-changing and all-engulfing Whole—be it the social or the cosmic totality." Not in resignation does he do so, but in a perverse love, "willing to make of his own total being, with all its values and standards and beliefs, an offering given . . . to that great Minotaur that is History." It is a monstrous self-denial, "paid for at the price of the very Self, and the existence and dignity of the human Person."

The great Minotaur that is History—a brilliant metaphor. Recall the myth. The Athenians had slain Androgeos, son of King Minos of Crete, out of envy for his athletic triumphs. Minos then demanded from Athens a yearly tribute of youths and maidens, to be shut in a vast labyrinth where dwelt the half-man half-bull Minotaur, conceived in bestial intercourse by Minos's queen. The Minotaur slew and devoured his yearly prey, until the hero Theseus came to town. He slew the Minotaur and, with the help of a ball of string given him by the princess Ariadne, found his way back out of the labyrinth.

Where there is faith, there is liberty. The heavens are open, and man's life has an aim, transcending his corporeal makeup, the particularities of his culture, and the monetary exchanges he must make along the road. Where there is no faith, human choices, in all their mad variety, reel back into the dark woods, or into the inextricable error of the labyrinth. But the labyrinth is intolerable. We *must* be going somewhere. Then it is that the Minotaur is summoned from the depths.

His name may be Evolution, now worshiped as a god. We will hurl ourselves into the maw of evolutionary change, even by our own tools accelerating that change, breeding the Minotaur to which we sacrifice ourselves. Let man perish, that the superman—or whatever it will be—may stalk the earth. His name may be History, worshiped as a god. History is not the sum of free human choices. It is its own being. It possesses its own thrust. It will not be denied. We may then either go down into the maw rejoicing, having won the Minotaur's favor—being on the "right" side of History, which means no more than yielding to inevitability now defined as right—or struggle against it in vain, and be devoured anyway, while our fellow tidbits mock us and wag their heads.

The man truly free is not encumbered by what the theologians call the vice of human respect. He does what is right because it is right, not because it will win him glory. If it is wrong to submit one's conscience to the approval of a debased man, it is all the worse to submit one's conscience to the approval of a debased culture. What the worship of the Minotaur does, however, is to transpose the submission into a vague future, to soften our sense of the contemptible.

This is not the Last Judgment, when God will reveal all the evil we should like to have hidden and all the goodness we so foolishly ignored. That will but reveal *what is the case now*. But when History is god, then one must take pains to flatter it, to align oneself with what one supposes people will say in a thousand years, knowing that those people will not be impartial judges either but will be formed by the inevitable and irrefragable historical process. It is to pimp oneself for the ages.

I cannot express the irony more trenchantly than Maritain has done. The rupture of the man without God, he says, "began as a claim to total independence and emancipation, as a proud revolutionary break with everything that submits man to alienation and heteronomy. It ends up in obeisance and prostrate submission to the all-powerful movement of History, in a kind of sacred surrender of the human soul to the blind god of History."

Here I might call up the great false prophets of the past, but that is not my point. It is not just that they guessed wrong as to where the bus was going. It is that they boarded the bus at all. Man without God is a commuter at best, or a tourist, or a prisoner; they amount to the same thing in the end. Only with God is he a pilgrim, and free. Every Minotaurian worshiper of the immanent drive of History has had it wrong. The Roman Empire is dust. The "dictatorship of the proletariat" is a bad joke. Manifest Destiny does not look so manifest. Revolutionaries are as common as weeds. They are not saints. It is the saints who are the revolutionaries.

The saints are free, in the most deeply human meaning of that word. Scrooge believed in Progress, and Scrooge sat hunched over his money and his accounts, reckoning up the debts of other men as if they and he were not fellow travelers to the grave, and beyond. Scrooge obeyed the law, which hardly pinched his actions. But Scrooge was not free. He was a sinner, sure enough, which is another way of saying that he was huddled up in himself, grasping and clutching. He could not fling himself away in love.

That was what Saint Francis did in the piazza of Assisi, when his father threatened to disown him before the bishop. The good boyish fellow flung away all his clothing and disowned his father instead. He said, in effect, "I will *not* submit myself to the Progress of the Family Bernardone. I will *not* pay homage to the changing times. I renounce the world, to love the world." And Francis went forth and preached, immersing himself in the love of God and neighbor and the beautiful things of creation. Caesar Augustus boasted that he found Rome in brick and left it in marble—mainly in marble false-fronts an inch thick. Caesar Augustus is in his tomb. The song of Saint Francis still resounds.

That harried fellow on the commuter train into the city, staring at his telephone, caught in the vortex of buying and selling, or of political advertisement, of important opinions, of books on the cutting edge—he is not the revolutionary, no matter what party he belongs to. He is not free, no matter how much power he appears to wield. The saint-in-making (I hope it is you, my reader) who retires to his closet to pray in secret, and to lose himself in the contemplation of God, is free. The man who organizes his "public service" according to the dictates of Progress, or whatever the Minotaur's name may be, is of all men most miserable, since not all his money or his sweat can buy him love, his own or another's. He bleeds himself dry along the road to the Minotaur. He misses the love of the saint and the pleasure of the sinner. But the man so caught up in the love of God that when he gives, his left hand does not know what his right hand is doing, he is truly free—so free of himself and with himself, he can hardly stop to notice how free he is, just as a healthy man does not think of his health and a man seized by joy has no idea of the radiance that glows in his countenance.

And when people accuse us of being retrograde, or medieval, or puritanical—all words rummaged out of the box labeled "Not Progressive"—we should shrug, as if they had accused us of walking on two feet, and smiling at the birds, like Saint Francis. If they like the locomotive so much, then all the better for them if we leave them an extra seat on it. Unless, that is, they envy our liberty. Let them envy it, then—and join us at last.

8

Fleeing the Family

The Orphan

Honor thy father and thy mother, as the Lord thy God hath commanded thee; that thy days may be prolonged, and that it may go well with thee, in the land which the Lord thy God giveth thee.

—*Deuteronomy 5:16*

To be attached to the subdivision, to love the little platoon we belong to in society, is the first principle (the germ as it were) of public affections. It is the first link in the series by which we proceed towards a love to our country, and to mankind.

—*Edmund Burke,* Reflections on the Revolution in France

I don't know whether the Welsh have preserved a love of home and hearth more tenderly than have their English neighbors. If they have, it may be one of the hidden blessings of unimportance. For the Important have to keep up appearances. They have to make sure that the stage lights are shining upon them, and then they have to mug and pose and strut upon that stage, sweating under the lights and the glare of spectators, who for their part shout sometimes for admiration and sometimes for envy and hatred. He who lives by the stage must live *on the stage* and die there, too. It's specified in the contract, signed in blood.

But nobody ever said that the sun did not set upon Greater Wales. Nobody ever said that Swansea was a shining city upon a hill. College students do not flock to Cardiff to see the coal mines. So it may be— the heart may hope—that there are homes in Wales, homes for the freedom of the human heart. Here, as I hear it, is a hymn to freedom. I'll try to translate it as literally as I can, keeping the gentle music:

Huna, blentyn, ar fy mynwes,	Sleep, little child, upon my bosom,
Clyd a chynnes ydyw hon.	Snug and warm my bosom is.
Breichiau mam sy'n dynn amdanat,	Mother's arms are tight around you,
Cariad mam sy dan fy mron.	A mother's love is in my breast.
Ni chaiff dim amharu'th gyntun,	Nothing shall disturb your slumber,
Ni wna undyn â thi gam;	There is no one shall do you harm;
Huna'n dawel, annwyl blentyn,	Sleep in quiet, dearest child,
Huna'n fwyn ar fron dy mam.	Sleep sweetly upon your mother's breast.
Huna'n dawel, heno, huna,	Sleep tonight in quiet, sleep,
Huna'n fwyn, y tlws ei lun;	Sleep sweetly, lovely you are to see;
Pam yr wyt yn awr yn gwenu,	Why is it now that you are smiling,
Gwenu'n dirion yn dy hun?	Smiling tenderly to yourself?
Ai angylion fry sy'n gwenu	Is it the angels above are smiling

Arnat ti yn gwenu'n llon,	Upon you in your smile of joy,
Tithau gwenu'n ôl dan huno,	And you return their smile, asleep,
Huna'n dawel ar fy mron?	Sleeping quietly upon my breast?
Paid ag ofni, dim ond deilen	Don't be frightened, it's just a leaf
Gura, gura ar y ddôr;	Tapping, tapping at the door;
Paid ag ofni, ton fach unig	Don't be frightened, a small lone wave
Sua, sua ar lan y môr.	Whispers, whispers on the shore.
Huna, blentyn, nid oes yma	Sleep, little child, it's nothing there
Ddim i roddi iti fraw;	That can bring you any fear;
Gwena'n dawel yn fy mynwes	Smile quietly upon my bosom
Ar yr engyl gwynion draw.	At the angels yonder, robed in white.

Yes, it is a lullaby. Sung to its melody *Suo Gân*, it enters the soul, finds a clean space there, and settles in, never to be wholly forgotten.

Let us now meditate upon this song.

We could notice how skillfully the poet has woven a few words, over and over, into the fabric of the song: *sleep, sweet, smile, quiet, angel, breast, child*. It is quite well done, and in the Welsh the words echo one another too. We could also comment upon the simple drama of the poem. For something does happen: the baby smiles in his sleep. That prompts the mother to ask why, and to suggest an answer. The baby is smiling at something that he can see but that we cannot. It is as if the baby were still near to that great and secret world whence he has recently arrived and could know its beauty without words to express it. The mother suggests that that must be it, and so through the baby she, too, is a part of that world.

But it is the reality and not the expression that moves the heart.

Outside of that scene, with the mother and the sleeping child, and the woman's bosom gently sustaining him in warmth and sweet repose, outside of that circle of grace, I cannot tell what can compare in importance. One might well feel that all the galaxies have burst into being only so that, somewhere on a green hillside in Wales, a mother should comfort her little baby by singing a song and be so immersed in wonder herself that she must repeat, over and over, her favorite words, *sleep, sweet, smile, quiet, angel, breast, child.*

Wales is not swallowed up in the universe. The universe offers its gifts to Wales.

In the quiet wonder of that Welsh mother there is no hurry. I am sure that mothers in old Wales had plenty of things to do to keep their families fed and warm and clean. But the mother here shows not the slightest inclination to do anything but to hold her baby upon her bosom, to gaze in wonder upon him, to talk to him even though he is asleep, to assure him, to sing to him, and to praise him. What about all the other necessities of life? What of the compulsions?

There are other things in the world below. But the mother says, twice over, *paid ag ofni*—don't be frightened. It's only a rustling leaf outside the door. It's only a little wave lapping upon the sands. The leaf cannot break in. The little wave cannot flood the land. It isn't that mother and child are huddling in temporary safety against the cruelties and compulsions of the outside world. Mother and child *are* the world, and are strong and safe. Those other things are small.

But the angels, dwelling beyond and deeply within the real world—that is, the world of the mother and the child upon her bosom—bring peace.

That lullaby presents a scene from the beginning of life. We turn again to Wales for a meditation on the end of life. I do not claim that this is great poetry. I claim that it is *good* poetry, not only well done but also good for man, good for his soul. It is in love with the goodness of home:

I am dreaming of the mountains of my home,
Of the mountains where in childhood I would roam.
I have dwelt neath southern skies,
Where the summer never dies,
But my heart is in the mountains of my home.

I can see the little homestead on the hill;
I can hear the magic music of the rill.
There is nothing can compare
With the love that once was there
In the lonely little homestead on the hill.

I can see the quiet churchyard down below,
Where the mountain breezes wander to and fro.
And when God my soul will keep
It is there I want to sleep,
With those dear old folks that loved me long ago.

One must have abandoned all humanity not to understand this simple poem. And that warrants some thought.

I grew up in a place that looked a little like the coal and slate country of Wales, though it was not nearly so rugged or beautiful. But I might have grown up on the plains of Kansas and beheld the vast starry sky above me in the winter, with thousands and thousands of stars that people who live in a city never see. Or I might first have heard the song of my mother in a flat in south Philadelphia and remember what it was like to sleep on a summer night out on the fire escape, and I might name the people who lived above us and below us and across the alley. The song is not just about one simple and beautiful place in Wales. It is about all simple and beautiful places that people have called home.

When husband and wife set down their stakes and build a home—not a residence but a home—they create a little world, one that, in their children, brings new life to generations past and opens that new life to generations to come. See the pictures. Here is a great-grandfather who has gone to another world but still abides with us; here are the little children now grown to dandle little children of their own upon their laps; here are those children, just born, now growing long in the limb, with shocks of tousled hair and mirth in their eyes. Every true home is as broad as Kansas, as rough and rumpled as Wales.

In a good home, a true home, people do not merely eat and sleep, or pursue their private interests behind closed doors; they *dwell* with one another and for one another. A home is like a church, as G. K. Chesterton would put it: bigger on the inside than on the outside. The farther you fly, comet-like, from the gravitational pull of home, the more you must submit to all the arbitrary edicts of the social machine.

That is the lesson of *David Copperfield*. Within the home, young David can enjoy the delights of life with his naive mother and their trusty maidservant, Peggotty:

> The first objects that assume a distinct presence before me, as I look far back, into the blank of my infancy, are my mother with her pretty hair and youthful shape, and Peggotty with no shape at all, and eyes so dark that they seemed to darken their whole neighbourhood in her face, and cheeks and arms so hard and red that I wondered the birds didn't peck her in preference to apples.
>
> I believe I can remember these two at a little distance apart, dwarfed to my sight by stooping down or kneeling on the floor, and I going unsteadily from the one to the other. I have an impression on my mind which I cannot distinguish from actual remembrance, of the touch of Peggotty's forefinger as she used to hold it out to me, and of its being roughened by needlework, like a pocket nutmeg-grater.

The young David here toddles from love to love. In one person that love is his mother, Clara, a young widow, weak, impressionable, but most dear to him, whom she loves entirely. In the other person that love is Peggotty, lumpish in body but true as touchstone in heart, the roughness of whose finger is but a sign of her devotion.

But Clara marries the villain Murdstone and dies brokenhearted after he dismisses Peggotty and sends David far away to a boarding school. Having destroyed the home (though he inherits the house), Murdstone reallocates his human asset, sending David to work in his bottle factory in the bowels of London:

> Murdstone and Grinby's trade was among a good many kinds of people, but an important branch of it was the supply of wines and spirits to certain packet ships. I forget now where they chiefly went, but I think there were some among them that made voyages both to the East and West Indies. I know that a great many empty bottles were one of the consequences of this traffic, and that certain men and boys were employed to examine them against the light, and reject those that were flawed, and to rinse and wash them. When the empty bottles ran short, there were labels to be pasted on full ones, or corks to be fitted to them, or seals to be put upon the corks, or finished bottles to be packed in casks. All this work was my work, and of the boys employed upon it I was one.

Twelve hours a day, for a pittance, young David works among hard-bitten boys and men, the offscourings of society. He is miserable. We should not think that the misery comes from the mere fact of work alone. Boys on a farm must do plenty of work. It comes from the kind of work, the place, the bad companions—and from all that is missing. It comes from *not being home*. Young David is not houseless. He has a roof over his head, in the boardinghouse he shares with Mr. Micawber. He is *homeless*.

The primacy of home: that is not merely one concern for that greatest of our English novelists. It is his heart and soul.

Outside of the home, the clock is the everlasting guard. Like as the waves make towards the pebbled shore, so do commuters hasten to their jobs. We wish the hands of the clock would move faster—we wish to *get through* the day. The best of days are those that pass so quickly, we seem to have arrived at the blessed hour of dismissal just after lunch—best unless we are behind in our work, so that the guard comes with his prod, snarling, "Hey, you! What are you doing? Composing an epic? Get a move on! Look what *time* it is!"

Outside of the home, time passes, time flies, time crawls. But inside the home, time can burrow down into *being*. When you are home, you are home. You need not *go anywhere*, and therefore you can, in imagination, in silence, in love, in freedom, go where you will and how you will. We can paraphrase Emily Dickinson: there is no frigate like a *home* to take us far away.

You can take a shovel and turn it toward the hill behind the back door, and make it into terraces, and use the rocks you pried up to bank up the terraces with walls, and carve out a maze of ditches, and plant tomatoes, beans, peas, corn, cucumbers, radishes, onions, carrots, peppers, squash, melons, lettuces, zinnias, marigolds, and petunias. You can sit on the porch with *The Last of the Mohicans* and sidle noiselessly through the woods of New York with Natty Bumppo. You can sit on the porch and play pinochle with the man next door. You can sit on the porch and look at the noonday sun. You can sit on the porch.

Inside the home, there are cisterns full of quiet. Oh, certainly not always! There is merry noise, often wrangling and grouching, a lot of idle chatter, some laughter, and some tears. There are certainly many things to do. But there is no railroad schedule. Inside the home, there is the possibility—no certainty, but always the possibility—of entry into a world whose moments are measured not by the movement of a mechanical hand but by the sway of a rocking chair, the ripples of easy conversation, or the mysterious rise and fall of human breath.

Freedom and the Home

The reader may conclude that I praise the home because there one is *free from* the network of arbitrary constraints that make a civil life possible. Home, then, would be the place where one can drive on the left hand side of the road, lie on the roof in the sun, and pray at any time of the day without inviting stares. There is something to that, but that's only a small part of what I mean. Again, we must resist the assumption that freedom is a negative, that it lacks substance.

When the pilgrim Dante attains to the highest reaches of Paradise—that is, the profoundest mystery of God revealing Himself to the human mind and heart—he returns "home," again and again, to say what he cannot say. "My words," he says, "are less than those of a small child who wets his tongue still at his mother's breast." It is not an idle comparison. We are brought again to the world of the mother and the child, and the material and spiritual act of love that unites them. We recall the mother Mary, and the Word made Flesh, the infant Jesus. What Dante means is that he cannot speak of the glory he has seen. But, then, no one can properly speak even of the glory of mother and child. Giotto's Mary, in the Scrovegni Chapel, gazes intently upon the swaddled babe, whose eyes meet hers. Some pictures are worth a thousand words; a thousand thousand words cannot exhaust the reality of that moment, as every mother knows.

Words fail us. They are like keys; they open, but they also shut. When we were small and could hardly raise ourselves from the floor, we curled our fingers round the fingers of mother and father, and we looked into their faces as they looked into ours. Where is the word for that? I am not saying that we then ignored the great big world around us. I am not saying that we were a little world unto ourselves. I am saying that during those times a boundless and mysterious world opened itself in our midst, as if suddenly we might become aware of another dimension, one of intensity and spiritual depths. All the rest of the world is flat; only in that world of love do real persons enjoy the room, infinite room, to live and move and have their being.

My father's body has returned to the dust; my mother is thin and shaky on her legs. But in my mind I see her pottering about the kitchen, singing to herself, while I am lying on the parlor floor a few feet away in our tiny home, drawing pictures on the cardboard that my father brought back with his shirts from the cleaner's. My sister is in the playpen, patting a red, white, and blue ball. We kept that silly ball for a long time. The pictures I am drawing are comic strips, of a rabbit and a bear, complete with speech bubbles and question marks and exclamation points. No schedule looms over my head. Another person, too, is present in the house, though only my mother knows it. It's my brother, in her womb. My sister plays herself to sleep. I turn to my picture book filled with stickers of animals that my mother has gotten from the grocery store. Each sticker has the name of the animal, its Latin species and genus, and a short description of where it lives and what it does. My favorites are the dinosaurs: *triceratops, stegosaurus, diplodocus.* I have them memorized without trying.

They mean more to me because my mother brought them. I am very small and dwell in complete dependence upon the love of my mother and father. I can smell the shoe polish under the kitchen sink, the shiny sticky stuff my father and I buffed on our shoes on Sunday morning. I can taste the burnt crusts of French toast soaked in maple syrup that my mother made for me sometimes. I can see the ragged old red sofa on its funny stumps for legs. I can read the nursery rhymes on the peeling linoleum of my bedroom floor, where my sister and I slept in one bed, and then where my sister and I and my brother slept in two bunks, me on top and the two of them below. I can hear the whistle of the now defunct Delaware and Hudson train on the opposite mountain of our town.

Why are such early memories especially strong? People will say it is because the small child has nothing else to think about, and so everything he encounters will strike him as wondrous. Inadequate explanation. First, everything is indeed wondrous; the child sees things only as they are. But *the things are filled with meaning, because they spring from a world of love.* In a few months I would go to kindergarten, afternoons for the spring. I remember a red brick building, a blackboard, the name of the teacher, and nothing else—nothing except my mother waiting for me outside on that first day. I did not want to leave home. I have almost no memories of first grade or of second grade. I find that, outside of the freedom opened up by love, my mind is a blank. I know *that* things happened, but it is as if they happened to only a piece of me, or as if they struck the skin but not the soul. It is as if I had temporarily left the real world and was made to inhabit a simulacrum of a world, where I was not really myself but a simulacrum of myself.

Systematic Alienation

And perhaps, if I were a child now, it would be something worse than a simulacrum.

Another scene, not in Wales.

The Controller is paying a visit to a school full of adolescent boys. He is confirming in them all the "freedoms" of their radically new education:

> Mustapha Mond leaned forward, shook a finger at them. "Just try to imagine it," he said, and his voice sent a strange thrill quivering along their diaphragms. "Try to realize what it was like to have a viviparous mother."
>
> That smutty word again. But none of them dreamed, this time, of smiling.
>
> "Try to imagine what 'living with one's family' meant."
>
> They tried; but obviously without the smallest success.
>
> "And do you know what a 'home' was?"
>
> They shook their heads.

When George Orwell wrote *Nineteen Eighty-Four*, he was not making a prediction. That's what some smug commentators happily made him out to have done when 1984 came round and there was still something called England and something called the United States of America. Orwell was making an observation. He based his Ministry of Truth, the place where historical fact is altered and precious evidence of the past is sent down a "memory hole" to be incinerated, on what he saw when he worked for the British Broadcasting Corporation. His satire was the modern world writ large.

The same is true of Aldous Huxley, from whose novel *Brave New World* I have taken the passage above. He was not predicting that these things would happen in some nauseatingly hygienic England of the future. He was confirming that these things were *already* happening.

The boys to whom the Controller is speaking were never born. They were *decanted*, as embryos, from their bottles, and were subjected methodically to such stimuli as would fit them perfectly for predetermined roles in a thoroughly managed world, one with complete sexual license and complete political subjugation of the individual to the state—and, therefore, one with no families. That is because the family can thrive only when the sexual powers are restrained and disciplined and held accountable to those realities that toddle about and are called "children." Therefore the family, since the time of Plato, has ever and correctly been seen as the first thing to be eradicated if the state is to assume its godlike role. *Mother* is the smutty word to which Mustapha Mond refers.

Of course they were not decanting British babies when Huxley was writing. They are not yet decanting them now. But think again of that intimate moment between mother and child. Or think again of the quiet time when you were a boy or girl (if, reader, you have indeed known that time), not harried from pillar to post, but simply *being*, in the company of the man who begot you from his loins and the woman who bore you in her bosom. Now let us begin to enumerate the things that have intruded, to shorten the duration of this blessed time, to make its moments irregular and then scarce, to adulterate their purity, to disrupt their living silence, to distract and disintegrate, to uproot and supplant.

The first commandment of Life Under Compulsion comes garbed in the robe of the deliverer. It says, "Thou shalt do as thou wilt," which is as much as to confess that nothing we want has any meaning other than what we happen to assign to it. And just as the old first commandment given to the children of Israel on Mount Sinai, "I am the Lord thy God," was bound to the first commandment of practical moral virtue, "Honor thy father and thy mother," so the new first commandment is bound to the new first commandment of practical oblivion: "Thou shalt be an orphan, in spirit if not in fact." And as the old commandment requiring filial piety implied that parents for their part would care for their children and bring them up in a godly and loving way, so now the new commandment implies a new mission for the parents: "Abandon your children, or so much the worse for you in your workplace or on the exchange." The old commandment came with a promise, in the land of milk and honey. The new commandment veils a threat, in the land of baby formula and plastics.

Now if the father cannot provide for his children, and if his countrymen are not willing to support him in his need, then the mother must earn a wage. Against her natural inclination she must leave the child. Love alone cannot put food in the belly or steam in the radiators. A merciful society would see to it that that happened as infrequently as possible by encouraging the formation of stable families, with fathers strongly committed to their wives and their children. We should want the father in the family so that the mother can be with the infant. We want the real freedom that the family brings.

But the Life Under Compulsion will have none of it. The first thing to do, then, in making orphans of us all is to remove as many fathers as possible. Bind the strong man, then take the house.

The easiest way to bind the strong man? Delilah knew. Craze him with what used to be called effeminacy, an untoward need to gratify his appetites. Sex does more than sell. It makes cravens of us all. In Huxley's novel, its grubbiest form is "sex-hormone chewing-gum." Our forms now are no finer. Men who have been taught, from the time they were small boys, that virility is all about sexual "performance," including frequency of release, will be unconcerned with self-denial, chastity, fidelity within marriage, and the careful moral upbringing of children. They will never outgrow a puerile fascination with their physical equipment. Look at the "men's" magazines and see whether you can find even one article on manly integrity, to be a straw in the balance against three hundred pounds of weightlifting, hormone pumping, sex seeking, and admiring oneself in the mirror.

Make men worthless and women won't have them. That is not a crack in the door. It is a wrecking ball through the roof.

Or maybe the women will have them, or a series of them, making matters all the worse. Return to the scene in that old Welsh lullaby. The mother can sing, "Don't be frightened, it's just a leaf, tapping, tapping at the door," because there is a house, solid and strong, and a father who has built it with his hands and who supports it with his labor and protects it with his watchful presence. The angel of the Lord came to Joseph, speaking to him in a dream and directing him as to how to protect the mother and the child. Joseph would go so far as to take them to Egypt, perhaps to his fellow Jews in Alexandria, to flee the jealous wrath of the bloodthirsty Idumaean pretender, Herod.

Now imagine the scene again, but it's not a leaf at the door or a little wave breaking upon the beach. It's the shadow of a large male creature, pacing, looming over mother and child. The child is not his. The child is his, but he did not want it. The child is his, and he thought he wanted it, but he wants something else even more. He has been taught nothing but to gratify his desires when he can, however he can. He has made no gift of himself—a gift which by the nature of mankind must be irrevocable—to the woman. He has begun to grow impatient with her attentions to the child. She has begun to grow weary of him. The shadow falls upon the child and stops there. "Put him to bed already," the male thing growls.

He has not been taught the high calling of a father. But has she been taught the high calling of a mother?

Return to the child at the mother's breast. This time she is not singing. She hasn't learned any songs. She is impatient with the child. One hand cups the child's head listlessly, while the other clicks the button on a remote control, changing the channel on the television. "Nothing's ever on," she says. She changes the channel. She changes the channel. She changes the channel.

There's a large boy sitting on the sofa across the room. Strange noises of projectiles and explosions sputter from the video game he is playing. He is bored by it. He glances over to the mother and child. The child is his. A part of him is waiting for the clock to go round the hour so that he can say honestly that he has spent enough time there. He glances toward the window. Another part of him eyes the mother askance, because he knows that she is not doing "her job," and that nettles him all the more because he does not even know what "his job" is. No one has told him.

"Quit fooling around with the TV," he says, crossly.

"Mind your own business," she replies. The baby wakes up and starts squalling. "Now see what you did!"

The female thing then hunches over the baby, making gurgling noises and raising her shoulder to close the male thing out of the scene. She will do so intermittently for the next year or so, until the novelty wears off the doll.

Have I exaggerated? I have not yet begun to weep.

Shadows on the Wall

Consider, one after another, the shadows that intrude upon that scene in the home. I shall let them speak for themselves.

"I am the Shadow of the Scalpel. A new life is valuable not in itself but only insofar as it gratifies you who must bear it. You need not have borne this child. You conceived it by accident. You did not *really* believe that the child-making thing would make a child. If you plant a seed in the ground, how often does it grow? It was a fluke, a freak. Well, you have done more than your duty. He's alive. But he doesn't have the right to mess things up for you worse than he's already done. You're not a saint. You're not a martyr. *He will have to make it up to you, somehow.*"

"I am the Shadow of the Empty Bed. You cannot be alone. You will not be able to bear it. Already you saw him looking at that blonde tart in the diner. This baby is in the way. You can't let it stay in the way. You have to win him back and tie him down. You have to do it to take care of yourself first. You'll be so lonely, so lonely."

"I am the Shadow of Glamour. Look at you. Look at the dishes piled in the sink. Look at the stain of breast milk and spit on your new outfit. That won't come out. The dirty diapers are piled so high in the garbage that you don't want to open it and suffer the sickly-sweet stench. So now the garbage is piling in the hallway. Those specks of dirt on the floor are from mice—I'll bet any money they're from mice. You used to have dreams. You were going to be a dancer. You were going to be a professor. You were going to sell stocks. You were going to travel around the world. You were going to be somebody. Now you're nobody. You're a fat girl with a dumb kid and a worthless boyfriend. Somebody will have to pay for it."

"I am the Shadow of the Pack. Your friends have come to visit and play with your doll, but they get bored with it almost as fast as you do. They tell you about the party you missed. They drink whiskey and get plastered. You can't, because of the baby. They tell you about the faculty seminar you missed. They drink cheap white wine and compete with one another in making intelligent comments on avant-garde poetry. You can't, because of the baby. They are getting jobs, or at least they are sending in their résumés. You can't, because of the baby. You will be left behind."

"I am the Shadow of Life. I come to you from the screen. You must pay attention to me! You must! You can't help it. You have to see, you have to hear. Don't look at the baby! Look at me, look at me! Listen to me! I shout, I scream, I wail, I wheedle, I sneer, I laugh, I snort, I suggest, I entice, I mock, I distract, I pull your brain to pieces!"

"I am the Shadow of Shadows. I come to tell you that your life is over. It would have been better if you had gone to the doctor and smothered the thing while you had the chance. Too late now. You have no real friends. You are a real friend to no one. You do not know your next-door neighbor. You probably would not want to know your next-door neighbor. What was that knock on the ceiling? Your mother is two hundred miles away. Your father is two thousand miles away. One minute exhausts your prayers. Less than that exhausts your songs. You know no poetry. Your inner life, what is it? A slick of automobile oil upon a blacktopped parking lot. Even your rainbows are slimy. What's this flesh? Fantastical puff paste. A paper cage for an insect. Don't suppose that it *means* anything. Get this time over with. That is what time is for."

Have I exaggerated? Or have I amplified the voices so that they might be heard? When was the last time you heard that every law we pass, every ship we sail, every mine we dig, every tower we build, and every war we fight, we do so ultimately so that a woman can rock her child to sleep within the profound haven of steadfast married love? Has it not been the reverse? Have we not said instead that women should have children—if they feel like it—because we are going to need the lawyers, sailors, miners, construction workers, and soldiers? Have we not said, in deeds more clearly than in words, though in words also, that the bearing of a child is significant only if it contributes to those utilitarian ends? Have we not suggested that it is, at best, a temporary layover on a woman's flight from Boston to Los Angeles? And no layover at all for the man?

Distance Learning

We don't need to descend into the misery of complete dysfunction to see that the lives of parents and children are quite different now from anything that any generation of human beings has ever experienced before. I might say that the effect, and perhaps also the purpose, of much of what we do at work, in school, and at home is to place as much distance as possible between parents and children. Children are to become orphans who live with their parents.

Let's take things one at a time. Large houses used to be for large families, as small houses were also for large families who didn't have so much money. Now, when you drive into a new subdivision, with cookie-cutter mansions, you see something the world has never known. There's one such a few hundred yards behind the house where I grew up. That area used to be called "the Pole Lines," because telephone lines had once crossed there diagonally from one part of town to another, through woods and swampy gullies and over rocks heaped up by the old glaciers. It was a magnet for the boys in our neighborhood. There were no houses, but there were the remains of strip mines, heaps of coal, mounds of the coal flakes called culm, an old car rusting into the ground, the hull of a school bus, the stone remains of what must have been a power relay for the miners, enormous rocks, a forty-foot cliff, chips of red ash that I still don't know the composition of, a disused blacktopped road, a stream draining a bog, paths that led to nowhere, white birches, wild roses, blackberry brambles, and patches of blueberries in July. In short, an ideal place for kids to explore.

There were no houses then, but there were kids. Now there are houses, but there are no kids. I have walked around up there and seen one big expensive house after another, but never any children. I believe that the size of a house built in the past thirty years is in inverse proportion to the number of people who live in it.

Imagine a "house" the size of three city blocks, for a father, a mother, and a child. How could that possibly be called a home? The people would be occupying different postal codes. They would have to send messages to one another over the airwaves (as I hear they do, from one room or walled borough to another). But that is the purpose of the overbearing house. It is to keep people from having to see one another all the time.

Then we move from the size of the house to its style of construction. The old Roman basilicas, which became models for Christian churches, were designed to bring people together. There was a large open central space, for meeting people. There were rooms or alcoves adjoining it. There were baths below, for men and for women, rooms with hot water bubbling up from natural springs, then warm water, then good old bracing cold water. The basilicas were all-purpose public places for doing business, meeting friends, exercising, relaxing in the waters, playing games, whatever.

Consider, by contrast, the modern semi-orphanage. I am told that in many states you cannot adopt a child unless he will have his own bedroom. Strange indeed: the orphan must remain alone at night; he probably had it better in the orphanage, where he might whisper in conversation to the kid in the bunk above him till they fell asleep.

So we shut ourselves apart in our cubicles. But nature calls, and if for no other reason than that, we might leave those rooms and rejoin the human race. Or perhaps not: we now build houses in which each bedroom has its own bathroom, keeping people apart in that way also.

What about entertainment? People do need to have fun once in a while. It is dull to play chess against yourself. Surely then the semi-orphans can return to their parents? Surely the parents want their children back in full?

Well, no, not exactly. Each room is provided with its own screen, *so that each member of the semi-orphanage can remain as such,* pre-occupying himself with his own habitual source of gratification and boredom. Even what is still called the living room—for we do not lack all sense of irony—is provided with a very large screen, so that the members drawing out their long half-lives can sit together but not *be* together, directing their attention not toward one another but toward a banal situation comedy, beer, toothpaste, hormone pills, and assorted other vulgarities and stupidities. I'm not saying that families can never come together to watch a favorite show or a movie. But the proliferation of screens makes it less and less likely that they will do so, or that they will even want to do so.

All of these intrusions, distractions, and disruptions are but the manifestations, in the home, of what the child will encounter later on.

Or we may say that what the child encounters later on is a predictable extension of what has already been happening in the home. Think of the day-care center. It is like a temporary orphanage. It has the ameliorating effect of bringing the child, for once, into the company of other children. At least orphans in an orphanage are around children quite a lot. But, unlike the orphanage proper, the day-care center is a business arrangement, and relations among the children must be slight and temporary. There is no "life" in the day-care center as there develops in an orphanage—no memories, no traditions, no stories. The workers at the day-care center, unlike those at the orphanage, do not and cannot consider themselves as ersatz parents. They will not be cooking for them. In "extreme" day-care asylums they may insert them into bed. They will not be tucking them in, lingering in love, and helping the little unwilling customers to say their prayers. You do not help customers to pray. The workers have their own lives to live, the children come and go, and once the children are taken from them, almost all will be forgotten, like the snows of yesteryear, and their place mats will know them no more.

This is a new thing in the history of the world: that children should spend most of their waking hours among people who do not love them and who, after a little time has passed, will not remember their names. I am not blaming the people who run the centers, just as I do not blame people who forget the names of the dogs they have housed in their kennels. I am blaming the very idea of the thing.

I can hear the objection, "But these centers are *necessary* if the mother, or in some cases the father, is to go to work." If they are necessary, they are necessary evils. But most of the clients do not view them as such. They are seen as *liberating* the parent, for work, *from* the child. And that is a strange liberty indeed. It is a headlong race away from love, and peace, and the only real world there is. And it is paid for by subjecting the small child to clockwork and impersonality. Time to get up, time to eat, time to go to the center, time to nap, time for playing in the playground under strict supervision, time for everything but simply *to be*.

I take it as axiomatic that you cannot be free unless you have a rich and wondrous world to be free in. For the small child trained up on clockwork and impersonality, four walls indeed do a prison make. There's all the difference in the world between the center, or the semi-orphanage, and a home, for the home is as broad and as deep and as surprising as a world, and those other things are at best shallow imitations.

The center has no history. But every true home is filled with stories. Look over here at the photographs in the glass hutch. Here is the great-great uncle who came over on a ship from starving Ireland with two English pounds in his pocket and fourteen years on his back. What was it like to be that boy, alone on the ship, staring over the gunwales into the endless ocean, wondering whether he would ever see his father or mother again?

What was it like to be my grandfather, alone on a ship from Italy to New York, just a bony, broad-shouldered teenager, following his father, who had gone to make a new life in America? What was it like for that boy, who could not speak a word of English, to stammer out his complicated surname to the man at the registry at Ellis Island, *Catanzariti*, "of the man from Catanzaro," and to have it squeezed and squashed into *Conserette*, which he duly wrote from then on, thinking it was English? And he somehow made his way 150 miles inland, to the coal-mining borough in Pennsylvania where I am writing these words now, and where he was not alone.

He was no orphan when he arrived here, even though his father was somewhere in New York. He was less homeless in this scrappy seam in the Appalachians than I am in my neighborhood in Rhode Island, in the house where my family and I have lived for nearly twenty years. That is because dozens of his neighbors from the Calabrian village of Tiriolo had followed one another precisely to this place and no other. The ties of kinship and blood were like transatlantic cables. They came here, and they worked the mines, and they married, and they built their own houses, and they, or rather mainly the wives, made homes.

The world outside of the home is a network of functional connections. It cannot afford to be too personal, not with the way work is now organized. You do not want the teenager behind the counter at the fast-food joint to ask you about your children or what book you have been reading. That is why, where there are few homes but many places of work and consumption, you can feel alone among thousands. The feeling is true. You *are* alone among thousands. You seem to have a freedom stretching from one horizon to the other, but it is an illusion. You have license to move about; you can take a train from New York to Washington, and then another from Washington to New York. No one can stop you.

But you cannot take that ride on any *personal* terms. You cannot make it your own. You cannot sit on the floor of the train and play checkers with your child. You must suppress the fullness of your personality; that is the tacit condition laid upon you when you buy the ticket. If you walk down Third Avenue singing "Guide Me, O Thou Great Jehovah," you will get puzzled and even angry stares. Someone might call the cops. You will be breaking the unwritten rule that allows for the function of the street—the rule of impersonality, of merging into the faceless crowd.

Our freedom is a *personal* freedom only when, in it and through it, our persons may flourish, but that is so only in love. Even the hermits of old bear witness to this truth. The young Saint Anthony walked into a church one day and heard the Gospel account of Jesus and the rich young man, whom Jesus invited to follow Him, once he had sold all he had and given the money to the poor. The rich young man walked away disappointed, because he was bound by those many things. But Anthony did something else. He did what Jesus suggested. So did his younger sister. And then he went out alone into the desert to spend his life in prayer.

But he was not really alone. He did not want to be alone for its own sake. He was *with* his fellow Christians in his heart and soul, spending many hours of every day praying for them. He wanted not to flee love but to chase after it. That explains why people began to chase after him, thousands of them, and the beloved Anthony would preach to them, in all the rest of his 108 years. He was free.

File off the fetters, then, those invisible fetters that circumscribe the world. Come out of the world of compulsion, that vast padded cell. Come home.

9

Giving In

The Mob

It's night, on the shores of the Thames. Two men are speaking in secret about the great question of the day, the matter of the king's divorce. In order to put asunder with legal impunity that which God had joined together, the king has broken with the pope in Rome and has declared himself to be the head of the Church in England.

But such a declaration will have no force unless you can compel people to honor it. You do this by various means, mainly by capitalizing upon fear, ambition, and greed. You compel by instigating compulsions. So King Henry seized manors, convents, monasteries, and abbeys belonging to the Church, most of them of venerable age and providing employment, alms, and medical care for villagers roundabout. He took them under the pretext that they were corrupt: even Henry had to pay vice's honor to virtue, which is hypocrisy. He knew that plenty of the nobility and the would-be nobility would smile at the seizure, because they could expect much of the proceeds to come their way. Think of it—our family, barons! Think of it—if you behave in a reasonable and agreeable way, if you bend the truth a little, if you perjure yourself in a manner friendly to the king, you can become the attorney general for Wales! And really, what choice is there? Better to make your peace with a bad cause than to lose your head, quite literally. And who knows that it really is a bad cause? Everybody else seems content with it. It is the wave of the future.

But there's one man who cannot go along to get along, because he knows it would be to tell a lie. The trouble is, he is Thomas More, the most learned man in England, and his very silence is deafening. So his friend the Duke of Norfolk is urging him to yield, for the sake of their friendship and to save his skin. Thomas says that their friendship must end, because Norfolk has a son. He does not want to put his friend's family in peril.

"You might as well advise a man to change the color of his hair!" cries Norfolk. "I'm fond of you, and there it is! You're fond of me, and there it is!" There's a hearty goodness in the duke, for all that he does not understand what is at stake. More acknowledges that fondness. What, then, is to be done? "Give in," says Norfolk, pleading. Give in. It is inevitable. You can't change things. Give in.

More knows he is going to disappoint his friend. "I can't give in, Howard." He smiles. "You might as well advise a man to change the color of his eyes. I can't. Our friendship's more mutable than *that*."

"Oh, that's immutable, is it? The one fixed point in a world of changing friendships is that Thomas More will not give in!"

Sir Thomas has to explain. This is not stubbornness. It is loyalty and devotion. It is as Jesus says, where a man's treasure is, there will his heart be also. If there is nothing fixed to which you devote your heart, or no One to whom you will to remain loyal forever, then you lose your very self. "To me it *has* to be," says Thomas, "for that's myself! Affection goes as deep in me as you think, but only God is love right through, Howard; and *that's* my *self*."

"You'll break my heart," says Norfolk.

And Thomas More will go to the scaffold, even cracking a jest for the occasion, and confessing himself to have been ever the king's good servant, but God's first.

The scene from Robert Bolt's screenplay for *A Man for All Seasons* reveals something fascinating about Life Under Compulsion. The Duke of Norfolk is not a bad man. He does not know whether the king's divorce is licit or not, because *he does not want to know.* He sees almost all the bishops going along with the divorce, and the bishops are learned men. He will accept any plausible argument put before him, not because he finds the arguments persuasive, since he does not really analyze them, but because they will serve well enough for the moment. The Duke of Norfolk is any duke, any burgher, any peasant, anywhere.

Suppose you had found the duke, alone, at the first moment when Henry decided that he must procure a divorce for the sake of dynastic succession and the pleasures of the bedchamber with Anne Boleyn. You put the question to him: "Howard, we will abide by your decision. You know how pious, gentle, and generous Queen Catherine has been, both at court and among the people, who love her. You know likewise what Jesus said about divorce. What do you say?" It is not likely that he would have dared to break with tradition, especially not if he had the countenance of the queen before his eyes. But it is often easier to compel a hundred people to do what you could never compel one person to do. The lone man must consult his conscience, that stern and unflattering arbiter. A man in a crowd, though, can turn to the others, as the others turn to one another, each justifying the deed by referring to the next man, or to the force of all the men together.

This is no new observation. The Italian novelist Eugenio Corti, dragooned into the army, fought on the Russian front, and there he beheld a dreadful spectacle, the Nazis and the communists fighting one another and wreaking unspeakable atrocities upon ordinary peasants. These were often peasants *from their own glorious fatherland.* He saw villages reduced to cannibalism. He saw trains stuffed full of prisoners, men and women and children crammed together in their own filth, freezing and starving, and sometimes devouring the flesh of the corpses among them. He saw the colossally stupid mistake that Hitler made, and that only a leader and a people fixed in the compulsions of evil could make. When the Germans breached the Russian border, says one of Corti's protagonists in *The Red Horse*, they could have taken the country, because "the Russians were hoping the

Germans would free them from communism." But instead of making common cause, the Germans "considered these poor wretches less than dirt, treated them any old way, continually threatening them and killing enormous numbers." Russian officers and soldiers for their part executed entire villages in both-sides-trampled Poland, murdering hundreds at a clip, firing shots to the back of the head.

After the war, the communists could not rest still—they dared not rest still. Evil is disintegrative and thus *requires* concerted effort to remain intact; every breath of health is a threat. Another of Corti's Italians observes: "What a dirty business, when one couldn't live in peace, even with the war over! It was only the Nazis and the Communists who had this sickening compulsion of not leaving people in peace, even interfering with their home life. What damned evil people!"

We should like to believe that if we had been living in Germany or Russia at the time, *we would have resisted the evil.* "Lay not that flattering unction to your soul," says Hamlet to his morally compromised mother. Paul Elmer More, writing several decades *before* this paroxysm of madness, tells us quite frankly what we must expect if we do not go along with the mob progressing to the brink:

> The world is not contradicted with impunity, and he who sets himself against the world's belief will have need of all a man's endurance and all a man's strength. . . . [He] will find himself subjected to an intellectual isolation and contempt almost as terrible as the penalties of the inquisition, and quite as effective in producing a silent conformity. If a man doubts this, let him try, and learn. Submission to the philosophy of change is the real effeminacy; it is the virile part to react.

Such a man is like a firm rock in the midst of the waves. They batter the rock from all sides, they go their way, but the rock remains. The people will call him antiquated, medieval, benighted, intransigent. Let the people talk. Dante was exiled unjustly from Florence along with others in his political party, and when they proved to be base timeservers, he disowned them and made of himself, he says, "a party of one." Romano Guardini, surveying the moral and intellectual ruin that was Europe after the Second World War, wrote that we had entered the era of "mass man," that the individual was being submerged beneath phenomena of the masses, which did not rise to the status of a true culture. Mass man has no culture, no real home, no transcendent object of devotion, no aim but what is given to him in and through mass education, mass entertainment, and mass politics. He floats on the seas willy-nilly, like a jellyfish, without a mind and a North Star to guide him. He gives in, he goes along. He lives, easily and uneventfully, Life Under Compulsion.

Submerged in the Masses, Starved of Friends

Man is made for friendship. Guarantee him wealth, power, and physical pleasure, but no true friend to share it with, and the very riches will be horrors to him. His wine will be battery acid. The sound of the bedsprings will be like a violin bow sawing against his teeth. Says the villain Richard III, on the night before the Battle of Bosworth Field: "I shall despair. There is no creature loves me; / And if I die, no soul shall pity me."

We must have friends. A newborn child given food and drink will still die without love. "I call you not servants," says Jesus to the apostles at the Last Supper. "I have called you friends." Surely at that moment eleven men at the supper table felt a clutch in the throat. The twelfth, we remember, had already put himself on the right side of Jewish history. He was the one who would betray Jesus, with a kiss.

In an ordinary human life, there is no felt conflict between your individual personhood and the love that binds you to a home, a village, a family, and friends. That is because the individual is realized *through* relationships. We might say that a man without friends is not a man at all. The man who lives for himself is not an individual. He is a reject. Now, just as the isolated Richard and the isolated Scrooge are not really individuals, and just as the principle of self-will makes miserable atoms of us all, so too people who are submerged in a collective do not really have friends through that collective. The atom is a false individual, and the cell in the collective is a false friend. Nor does it matter what political dress the collective wears. In this sense, and not in a truly patriotic or religious sense, one uniform is like another.

Another scene. It's a barn, in Italy, during the rise of the Fascist regime. There are three men, a dog, and a donkey. None of the five creatures is wearing a uniform. One of the men, the young Pietro, a former Socialist Party member, is a young refugee from the law. His host is old Simone, called the Polecat for his habit of swiping chickens, and making restitution for them later on. The third man is a deaf mute whom Pietro has befriended. He is called Infante, meaning, literally, the man who cannot speak. Pietro has been teaching Infante how to say a few words. The shaggy dog, intensely loyal even when he has to suffer with bad food and cold weather, is named Leone—Lion. The donkey, old, arthritic, quiet, sad, immensely patient, is named Cherubino—the Cherub. Cherubino and Leone were the Polecat's best friends until Pietro came along, and the deaf mute.

They don't have much to eat or drink, but they have enough, and they have long nights of conversation, or quiet, just being with one another. The friendship of noble-born Pietro and the less-than-peasant Simone is as solid as rock. In fact, it brings Simone back into a world of friendships past:

> The presence of Pietro and Infante recalled to him faraway and long-forgotten friends, those of his early youth and of the time when he had emigrated to Brazil and Argentina. Where might they be and were they still alive? Were they too cowed and submissive? Simone himself was astounded by the clarity, the precision and the freshness of certain sudden memories, by the ease with which he could remember faces, smiles, ways of speaking,

names of persons and of places, dates and even the most trivial circumstances, for so many years buried in oblivion.

And he shares these with his friend. "Pietro," he says, "if only you had known Bartolomeo the dyer, from Celano; or, better yet, if only he had known you!"

The scene is from *The Seed beneath the Snow*, by Ignazio Silone, writing between the world wars. Silone was no conservative. He was a liberal of that rarest of kinds, one who has seen the emptiness of most of what passes for politics and who allies himself with the poor because, as his hero Pietro puts it, among them, with all their many sins and their narrowness of mind, there is at least the possibility of hearing the truth. We will add that where people cannot speak the truth, because the force of mass compulsions makes it dangerous or even inconceivable, there can be no real friendship. So Pietro says to his friend the Polecat in the barn, "I didn't have any real friends in the Party," though he had spent fifteen years among them and had worked with thousands. "I never knew a soul as well as I know you and Infante."

The particular nature of the party is not so important as is the party spirit itself, the compulsion to align yourself with a mass movement. Pietro is a man of the Left. While he and his gruff friends are talking in the barn, the "important" people in the town are waiting at a banquet for the new Fascist official to arrive, to curry his favor. The atmosphere is tense, because everyone in the dining room has been in the debt of the now cashiered official, and they are waiting to find out what their fate will be. Worse yet, the new official is late to arrive. "It was no laughing matter," writes Silone, "to be gathered together at a banquet for no good reason other than the common bond of being under suspicion. Every man looked at his neighbor as if the latter's presence were damaging in his own case; each one seemed to be saying to himself, 'Good God, what company I have fallen into!'"

The name of the new official is also telling: Marcantonio. We are meant to recall Shakespeare's *Julius Caesar* and the speech that

Mark Antony gave to the plebeians of Rome on the steps of the Senate house, turning them into an indignant mob and causing the republican assassins Brutus and Cassius to have to flee the city for their lives. Marcantonio's new position? Government *orator*: a corrupter of words, to move the masses; a man who tries to follow in the footsteps of the leader Mussolini by spritzing his exclamations with German.

While they are waiting for him, the judge Don Achille speaks up, with sly and devastating irony, saying that the whole history of mankind is the history of *rhetoric*: that is, the history of moving masses of people by words, words, words. That is all there is in Political Life Under Compulsion. Words are not troves of truth or bands of friendship. They are tools, and the people who use them are tools, and so are the people upon whom they are used. This is ultimately the meaning, says the Judge with breathtaking blasphemy, while a priest looks on and blandly agrees, of the verse in John's Gospel: *In the beginning was the Word*.

Why do people go along with such things? Why do they throw away their souls? It is the sad and inhuman parody of love.

Isolation Is an Illusion

"No man is an island, entire of itself," wrote John Donne in his most famous meditation upon death. "Every man is a piece of the continent, a part of the main." We pretend to stand aloof at the price of our very humanity. "Any man's death diminishes me," says the reverend, "because I am involved in mankind." There is a powerful metaphor submerged in that verb *involved*. Donne says that he is folded into mankind, enveloped by his fellow men, intermingled with their sorrows and their joys. When the bell tolls, then, it does not merely toll for a fellow townsman or a brother. Do not trouble to send for whom it tolls. "It tolls for thee."

Noble sentiments? Not so. It is reality, as solid as rock. Try to deny it. What happens? You can no more cut yourself off from mankind than you can stand on air. You must join them in love, freely given, or *be joined to them by compulsions, whether you like it or not*. And you will in the end not like it at all. You can fall down to your knees by their side, in humble prayer, or you can be hustled along with them in a mad crowd shouting slogans and beating the tin tops of garbage cans. For the mob is a congregation of compulsions. It does not matter who or what squats upon the altar: Robespierre, Beelzebub, Mussolini, Belial, any political or social savior with the sibilant speech and the slick tongue, hissing out every other word with its suffix -*ism*. The people will be saved not by the grace of God, not by any act of faith, hope, or charity. They will be saved *because they belong to the right mob*. They think they have pulled the lever of righteousness, but they are themselves the levers that are pulled.

A mob is not a great cloud of witnesses. It is not a gathering of friends for a wedding feast. It is a herd of enemies who have fused their enmity with the *cause*, whereof they are the willing effects. Witness the goings-on when a politician dies. No one, in Life Under Compulsion, says to himself, "The fearful reckoning he meets may be mine, soon." They turn the funeral into a political event. They *must*: they are marionettes and they will dance. They look over the shoulder to see who gets the prime time for the moist eye and the hitch in the voice. They work out a calculus of advantages. One hypocrite leers at another. The man who still retains a shred of decency feels he is being outflanked by the more ambitious. "Whatever I really believe," he says, "the game is what it is." He plays along. He becomes one more organ grinder. He locks himself into the compulsion.

"And if I die," says Richard, "no soul shall pity me." Does it matter, really, whether the survivors feel glee at your grave site or feel nothing but excitement at the opportunity for advancement in the mob? What is the friendship that the mob, or the mass phenomena, cannot give?

C. S. Lewis, in *The Four Loves*, sets us on the right track. "Friendship," he says, "arises out of mere Companionship when two or more of the companions discover that they have in common some insight or interest or even taste which the others do not share and which, till that moment, each believed to be his own unique treasure (or burden)." Notice: what they share is not something idle but a great treasure, or a great burden. They love the novels of Tolstoy. They suffered the loss of a father when they were boys. They lose themselves in wandering the hills in search of rare flowers. They have a passion for raising prize roosters. Like Silone's Infante, Simone, and Pietro, they are shunned by the Very Important, the politicians. The bond between them is forged by a prior bond. They give their hearts to one another because each has already given his heart to something else.

"It is when two such persons discover one another," says Lewis, "when, whether with immense difficulties and semi-articulate fumblings or with what would seem to us amazing and elliptical speed, they share their vision—it is then that Friendship is born. And instantly they stand together in an immense solitude." That solitude, though, is not the same as isolation or loneliness. It is like the quiet plenitude of a clear night sky powdered with stars. It is far from the madding crowd. Within that charmed circle of friendship, you need not worry about who is winning which congressional seat, or what sleazy gown the latest famous actress wore on her inevitable slide toward old age and oblivion, or any of the other things that the mass phenomena shout into your ears or flash into your eyes.

"Did you hear something?" says Bob, flicking his fishing line farther out into the pond.

"Something from town, I guess," says Jim.

"I wonder what it was," says Bob, ten minutes later.

"Whatever it was, it's gone now," says Jim, easing his shoulders back against the side of the boat and pulling his cap over his eyes.

Or, as Kenneth Grahame's wonderful Water Rat says to his friend Mole, in *The Wind in the Willows*, "There is nothing—absolutely nothing—half so much worth doing as simply messing around in boats." There is a real world there. The birds twitter, the waves lap against the shore, the fish flurry about and nip at the line.

The thing is, we will have either one or the other. We will have the empty loneliness of the mob or the life of friendship. Another way of putting it is that we are made for heaven, but we can choose hell instead. To say, with Satan, that you are your own is to tell the same old dreary lie that hordes of indistinguishable sinners have said before you. Well did Dante show forth the phenomenon in his *Inferno*. Some of the sinners, it is true, retain a kind of single-minded individuality, standing forth in ruined grandeur. But most of the sinners are submerged into a pathetic subhumanity, at once isolated from one another and compelled to be near one another, even to be indistinguishable from one another.

So the souls of the opportunists, that great mob of moderates who commit to nothing, are stung by hornets and mosquitoes, their dripping blood gobbled up by maggots. They have no names. The souls of the avaricious and the prodigal roll great stones against one another, crying out against the other's vice. They have no names. The souls of the spiritually sluggish and sullen are submerged beneath the squalid waves of the Styx. They have no names. The souls of the worst of the traitors are fully encased in ice. They have no names. Even souls whose names we learn derive no pleasure from the proximity of their fellows. One of the ice-bound traitors describes a fellow traitor as the man whose head is in his way, to block his sight. Master Adam the con artist and Sinon the liar are within inches of each other, yet all they feel is hatred and contempt.

But when Dante reaches Purgatory, the first souls he meets are doing something far more delightful than messing around in a boat. They are *singing a hymn in a boat*, leaning forward toward the prow, looking forward to the mountain of their atonement and their reconciliation with God and with their fellow men. There is no compulsion among them but rather eager gratitude and love. They pray for one another. They pray with one another. They sing *In exitu Israel de Aegypto*: when from the land of Egypt Israel came. They rejoice because Christ has taken captivity captive and set their souls free.

In a pit of mud, everyone looks like everyone else. It is the clean who are distinct. In a mob, everyone behaves like everyone else. It is the friend who is distinct. In a movement of the masses, every face distorted with passion resembles every other—every tic, every compulsive spasm, every burst of chaos. It is the man in prayer, kneeling beside his friends, who is distinct. To that ultimate source and aim of freedom we now turn.

10

Fear of Contemplation

The Box

The creature itself also shall be delivered from the bondage of corruption into the glorious liberty of the children of God.
—*Romans 8:21*

I am looking at *Saying Grace*, an extraordinary painting by Norman Rockwell.

I've never caught the bug for despising beautiful things or dabbling in the hideous. I cannot, nor do I wish to, learn not to look in art for beauty, intelligence, consummate skill, human feeling, and truth. So I am looking at Rockwell's painting, and I don't care who knows it.

It's a cluttered, slovenly restaurant at a railway station. An old lady with a crumpled green old lady's hat—the daisy in front is a fine touch of freshness and open air in these stuffy quarters—sits at a table, her head bowed and her bony hands clasped in prayer. Her grandson sits beside her, his back to the viewer. He has close-cropped red hair and the tad-too-big ears that tug at a mother's heart. His head is bowed, too, and the set of his shoulders and arms suggests that he, too, has his hands clasped. He's leaning slightly toward Grandma. He has taken off his hat, a gray bowler with a small red cockade. It lies below with an umbrella and Grandma's bags. He looks very much like a little man, and that's quite right, because the other figures in the painting are men.

Those men are drawn to the scene of prayer. We don't know why. One of them, seated in the foreground, glances askance at them, a cigar in his left hand, a rolled-up newspaper on the table, with a saucer of cigarette butts and a plate full of the broken remnants of his lunch. He's laid his knife and fork across the remnants as if to say, "That's it, to hell with the rest." Another man, with a hard-bitten face, knits his brows and looks down at them, his mouth pressed tight in an expression that I can describe only as a grimace of distant approval.

But the really dramatic figures are the two young men who are seated at the same table with the grandmother and the grandson. One leans forward, clutching his coffee cup, as if caught by surprise. A cigarette dangles from his lips. The other, a reddish blond, and exceptionally good-looking but in a sad, transient sort of way, leans toward his friend while gazing at the couple in rapt attention. He could have been that boy, long ago. He is holding a cigarette in his right hand, and the smoke rises up in a thin white wisp between him and his friend.

On one side of the table, silent words and prayers rise up to God, in thanksgiving for the very ordinary meal. On the other side, moral embarrassment, and cigarette smoke.

There is not the slightest sense of ostentation in the grandma and the boy. Their bodies suggest they are for each other and for God. Yet in their simple piety they create a space of profound freedom. They are in the railway station, and not in the railway station. They are both comfortable where they are—they do not seem the least bit tense or wary or self-conscious—and they are going somewhere, while the men in the painting appear to have gotten stuck. In fact, the boy and Grandma seem to have forgotten themselves entirely, surely the sweetest freedom of all. If the men were not also struck in the heart, I might say that the lady and the boy had entered a den of thieves and turned it into a house of prayer.

What is it that people fear so much about prayer? When our schools were built to resemble the churches or the town halls of a free people, it was taken for granted that there would be prayer. What would a dance be without music? The spires were like jousting lances in a tournament against the sky. The people aimed high, because their hearts were high. They freely gave what they had freely received. They need not bow to any prince, to any system of government, to any worldly army, or to any cabal of men conspiring to clap them in bonds for the good of the state. To my mind there is nothing so free as a group of people, old and young, men and women and children, singing songs of praise from of old to the glory of God. "Prayer and sacrifice," says Chesterton, "are a liberty and an enlargement," opening up the soul of man to the infinite God and inviting Him to come and dwell among us, to have a local habitation and a name.

I think it is not accidental, then, that schools stopped resembling houses of prayer or the town halls of a free people, which is to say a people open to God, about the time when prayer was sent packing from the schools, *as if prayer were the prison and not the key, as if it were the cell and not the free heavens, as if it were the burden on the shoulders and not the promise of release, as if it were the cause of alienation and not of community.* And, at the same time, we began to build schools that are all inside and no outside, all stone and no garden, all power and no humility, all hulking system and no small child, all gears and no flowers, all compulsion and no promise. The face gives witness to the life or the death within.

Suppose the proprietor of the restaurant had said, "I do not want my customers to be *compelled* to witness a moment of prayer. It might embarrass them. Therefore this will be a prayer-free restaurant. No Saying Grace Allowed." Forget for a moment the small matter of civil license to think what you will and speak what you think. In what way could the restaurant possibly be held to be *more truly free* after the banishment of the public prayer?

In other words, remove the boy and his grandmother from Rockwell's painting. What is left?

A seedy diner at a railway station, that is what's left, and men abandoned to their compulsions. They smoke, they down coffees, they check the racetracks, they go to work they do not enjoy, they return to difficult homes, they hunt for women, they pursue whatever alleviates the weariness of a world with no heaven, which might as well be a world with no sky. But far away from the diner are men with the compulsion and the financial and political might to rule. For it is some consolation, if one must be whipped, to ply the whip oneself; in a terrible parody of the words of the Lord, it is better to give than to receive. Thus will the powers, set free from freedom, rule without constraint or scruples. It is absolutely astounding how many miserable compulsions a degraded people will tamely and timidly endure if only to be relieved of the threat of prayer. Having dwelt so long underground, they fear the open blue.

I have long been thinking that the only tonic for these sick people is the freedom shown by the old lady and the boy in the picture. It is the freedom of being entirely open to God and thus entirely open to man, open to the point of nakedness. Grandma and grandson are weak and vulnerable, in their forms and in their sweet freedom, but where I am weak, says Saint Paul, there am I strong. If people run from freedom, then let freedom stride happily into their midst. If people will not listen to reason, let them listen to song.

Faith in men is for slaves. Faith in man is for fools. Faith in God is for men.

Contemplation, Upon Earth

I am looking at another painting by Norman Rockwell, a part of his Four Seasons Calendar: *Grandpa and Me in Summer*. Again, I know that I am not supposed to enjoy paintings by Rockwell, because the man had skill and humanity and wit and grace and love, just when the philosopher critics have commanded us to pretend to enjoy what is mock-primitive, bestial, flippant, awkward, and mean. But I enjoy Rockwell nonetheless, just as I prefer an easy conversation with a sane man to an argument with a lunatic. Norman Rockwell is sane.

In this picture, Grandpa is lying on his back on a green slope, with his hands behind his head for a pillow and his hat pulled half-way down over his eyes. It's hard to tell whether he's dozing or not. It seems that he's in that blessed peace between a light nap and the calm refreshment of gazing up into the clear sky. A spray of scraggly birch leaves hangs over him from above.

The boy, meanwhile, is lost in another kind of contemplation. He's sitting in front, right next to Grandpa's side. His straw hat is set back to reveal his whole face. The legs of his patched trousers are rolled almost up to his knees, which are tucked up, while his bare feet, big bony feet, scuffed and dirty with life, brace against the hillside. His she-dog beagle nestles under a knee as she sniffs at one of the three yellow-paper butterflies flitting about. But the boy isn't thinking of the dog or the butterflies, or even Grandpa. He has a wild daisy in his hand—there are a few of them on the slope—and he's picking the petals off, one by one. "She loves me, she loves me not, she loves me . . ."—that is evidently what is in his mind, as he looks at the flower with the slightest trace of a smile on his lips and his eyebrows raised just a little, in wonder.

Someone asks me, "What is our life on earth for?" I would answer, "It is for life in abundance, before the face of God." But if he begged for a more proximate answer, it would be hard to do better than to point toward this picture and say, "It is for an old man, a dog, and a boy to sit on a hillside, the old man dozing and looking to the heavens, the dog happy to be in the free air, and the boy plucking the petals of a flower as he thinks of the girl he likes best."

I know that these are country people, and living in the country meant work. That's all right. The boy's ankles and calves are those of somebody who has done a lot of chores, and a lot of running and climbing and walking, too. The old man is a wiry, grizzled fellow, with wrists like leather straps. I'm not saying that all the mechanisms of civilized life exist so that people can have a vacation now and then. We desire not freedom *from work* but freedom in and through our work, freedom for the largehearted friendship and peace and wonder that Rockwell portrays in the painting. I go to an airport and I see people intent, stolid, perfectly frozen in their busy-ness; the old man gains more human good from his nap than they from their ergonomic tics. His treasure, if not in heaven, is in the sky, where tax men cannot tax nor moths consume. I go to a university and see people clambering up the greased pole of ambition, to be noticed, to publish in the best journals, to win a scrap of turf from their departmental rivals. But the boy is more philosophical than they. They are in love with phantasms. He is in love with a pretty girl.

Now there are two ways to ensure that a scene like this will be inconceivable. One is to make sure that the boy and Grandpa never have the opportunity to relax on the hillside in the summer sun. The other, more reliable, is to make sure that there are no boy and Grandpa to begin with. In the end, though, perhaps the two ways are really one. It is to raise up a generation of people who cannot be free. They have grown so used to the four walls that do a prison make that the open air, and silence, and the sky strike them with a vague terror. They prefer that the sky threaten, that they may have an excuse to get free of their freedom. They prefer the noise, lest they hear the still small voice that the prophet heard, who then hid his face in awe.

We could imagine the boy and Grandpa as our contemporaries. The boy would be sitting on the hillside with a dull, fidgety look, kicking at a rut. Grandpa would have his chin in his palm and his fingers over his nose and one eye, wondering why on earth his wife nagged him into taking a boring walk with a boring grandson on a boring day. And we could imagine the beagle, cocking her head with a half-whimper, half-growl, as if to say, "What is wrong with you two? Can't you smell the butterflies?"

But in Rockwell's painting, the boy and Grandpa are *free*. It isn't just that they are not straining their muscles. Freedom is the movement of the heart to embrace what is good, or beautiful, or noble. A man who cannot admire is a slave. The world is given to us gratis, and it will be taken only on those terms. We must be grateful to be free.

Then, if we don't want the scene that Rockwell painted, we must raise a nation of slaves. Freedom, how do we hate thee? Let me count the ways.

The boy likes a pretty girl. That is natural. It is foolish to say that he is "bound" by his boyish nature to notice girls. It is like bemoaning the fact that birds are sentenced to fly. So we must instill in him what is not natural, to make a slave of him. We have to clip his wings. We tell him that girls are tramps and show him some to prove the point.

The boy is comfortable in his thoughts. That is natural, too. It is foolish to say that he is "bound" by his thoughts. It is like bemoaning that fish have water to swim in. So we must batter the walls of his sanctuary, to let *other messages come in*, those of our devising. Advertisements, sublingual songs, blaring headlines, unnatural colors, crying, "Buy me! Consume me! Take me! Now or never! Loser! Loser if you don't! Buy! Look! Hey! Watch me!" It's what school is for.

The boy is at home with the old man. That is natural, achingly so. It isn't true that children like best to play with other children. They like best to play with old people, so long as the old people are children, too. It's as if the boy and the old man, in their matter-of-fact camaraderie, formed a fabulous beast indeed, one that would live to be three score and ten and three score and ten, with a pair of long legs and a pair of stubby legs, and a head addled by youth and a head addled by age, open to the wonder of just having come from eternity and to the wonder of being just about to return to it. It is not good for the old man to be alone, and that is why the Lord God fashioned him a grandson, poking him in the ribs and begging him to go for a walk into the everlasting hills.

So we must keep them apart. If there is no generation gap, we must open one up, and make it as wide as a continent. For this purpose we sow something more destructive than differences. We sow indifferences.

Do we live in a just and sane society? How many old men and boys lying on a hillside have you seen?

United from Above

"Where two or three are gathered together in my name," says Jesus, "there am I in the midst of them."

It is a mark of a narcissistic age that some Christians have come to interpret these words as suggesting that we *make* Jesus present by means of our community, when exactly the reverse is the case. The only reason why Christians gather is that Jesus has already united us. We gather not in our names but in *His name*. It is He who has called us out of the darkness of egoism into His wonderful light. Jews at Passover do not make God present in the cloud and the pillar of fire. They eat the Passover meal because God has already made Himself present among their fathers, whom He led from Egypt into liberty.

We are ever really united only from above, and not by our power but by our surrendering to the power of something that transcends us. This law holds true, as the philosopher Dietrich von Hildebrand shows, even for things in the natural order. "We must not forget," says he, "that values possess a unifying power; and the higher the value in question, the greater this power. In beholding a value, in grasping it, the soul of the individual is not only 'recollected,' drawn out of 'distraction,' but the barrier isolating him from other men is lifted." When two men of deep sensitivity listen to Bach's *Passion according to Saint Matthew*, distinctions of class and party melt away. If business rivals or brothers in conflict suddenly encounter an act of great heroism, their hard thoughts are taken from their hearts, and all division seems petty. They enjoy together the warmth of the goodness, as people brought out of a dank cave behold the sun, and behold one another by its light.

It follows that beauty and solemnity are not aesthetic attachments but are of the essence of the community-forming power of values generally, and of the art of common worship above all. If we attend a ball game, we may enjoy the good fellowship of other fans in the stands, and there's nothing wrong with that, but it is slight and transient. Contrast that with what Hildebrand, a Roman Catholic, says about the liturgy, which "combines holy sobriety with the greatest ardor, eternal calm with the deepest emotion, holy fear with holy joy, and winged peace." It can accomplish this because, though it employs our language and gestures and art, it is in its essence not ours but Christ's: "The Liturgy is Christ praying." In God alone are our particularities founded, and in Christ are they brought together in a communion of polyphonic praise and love.

Hildebrand gives us powerful examples of how this is so. Here I beg the reader to see beyond the specifics of Catholic worship to the general truth he is illustrating. Consider the words of Saint Paul that used to be heard in the epistle on Holy Saturday: "Mind the things that are above, not the things that are upon the earth. For you are dead; and your life is hid with Christ in God." *For you are dead*: the words strike with the shock of a fearful and mysterious revelation. We hear the service and expect to be dwelling upon the body of Christ in the grave in that dead time between the Cross and the stone rolled away from the tomb. But we hear more; we hear that we, too, are dead. We have died with Christ in baptism. We are dying to ourselves and the world. We must no longer mind the things that are below. We must no longer haunt the tombs by the roadside. The world misses it, but our life is hid with Christ in God, just as the first Easter was yet hidden in the earth, or rather hidden in the providence of the Father.

In other words, in the drama of religious faith, the words of one prophet or saint are brought into communication with other events, other human beings, and other works of God. It is not simply that the Old Testament foreshadows the New, and it is certainly not that the Old may be dispensed with. The drama elevates individuality and transfigures it. We recall that on the glorious mountain Jesus was seen alongside Moses and Elijah, and they from the Old Testament *were in conversation with Him*, exactly as the reading from the Old Testament, the psalm, the epistle, and the Gospel are placed in conversation with one another in the liturgy.

The spirit of that religious drama suggests that we do not become ourselves until we join the symphony. "An isolated man," says Hildebrand, "one who has not become conscious of the ultimate objective link binding him to all other men before God, is an unawakened, immature, even a mutilated man."

Think of the loneliness of modern man, who is encouraged to fall in prone adoration to the abstraction of choice—never mind *which* choice we make. Such a man may enjoy the company of others like him but not the deep friendship founded upon a shared reverence for something of transcendent worth, something that we do not choose but rather receive, as a wondrous gift. But "the fathers of the desert and the hermits lived entirely in that spirit of true communion," says Hildebrand, and the people sought them out, and they prayed for one another and commiserated and rejoiced with one another. Saint Simon, that extravagant ascetic on the pillar, was more deeply immersed in communion with God and with his fellow man, and was more fully a person, than are our "pagan contemporaries inhabiting crowded cities, surrounded by other men and bound to them by peripheral ties."

To affirm that we are united only from above, however, is not to affirm that the union occurs on the cheap. Consider the mystery of personal being. Hildebrand understands that even in the case of human friendship, there are stages that must be passed through, and this *discretion* is right and just. The man who knows only technological efficiency will not understand it but will want "to fabricate things brutally, from the outside, without any sense of the dramatic character of the being's unfolding itself in time." Even in friendship, the utilitarian makes shortcuts.

But there are no careless aisles to the Almighty. We do not—we should not—approach the Lord with thoughtless familiarity. Hildebrand recalls the words of the priest preparing for Mass, "I shall go in unto the altar of God, of God, who gives joy to my youth." He says those words even if his hair is white and his hand trembles. If we dwell within the drama of faith, then, falling to our knees as we confess that we are not worthy of so great a grace, we find ourselves in our self-forgetting, and we find our neighbor kneeling beside us.

Nothing to Celebrate and No One to Worship

Thee let old men, Thee let young men,
Thee let boys in chorus sing;
Matrons, virgins, little maidens,
With glad voices answering:
Let their guileless songs re-echo,
And the heart its music bring,
Evermore and evermore!
> —From Prudentius, Corde natus ex parentis *(fourth century), tr. John Mason Neale (1854)*

WINTER CONCERT 12/12
WINTER HOLIDAY BEGINS 12/21
> —From a sign outside of the Wakefield Hills Middle School, West Warwick, Rhode Island

To please my son, innocent of the cruelties of our time, we turned on the television a few minutes before midnight on New Year's Eve to see the "ball" in Times Square drop. There were a million people below, waiting for the inexorable flip of the temporal odometer. I'm not sure what they were celebrating, but the frenzy seemed proportionate to the triviality and impersonality of the moment. When the last tick of the clock arrived, the band played that song whose words nobody really understands, but which I will translate in a form fit for the age:

Let auld acquaintance be forgot
And never brought to mind;
Let auld acquaintance be forgot
With all the ties that bind.

Return to that lovely song by Prudentius, which in the self-forgetfulness of joy celebrates the birth of Jesus. Unlike the tick of the clock, the moment of Jesus's birth does not arrive in complete abstraction from all things most profoundly human, nor does it leave with the celerity of the second hand. It is not *secular*, in the deep sense of that word, suggesting one thing following upon another. It stands above the world; it beats in the heart of the world.

There's nothing hectic in the praise that Prudentius calls forth. All the ages of man are brought in communion, with the angels and the saints that have gone before us. All is cheerful, wondering, solemn, and gladsome at once. It is *free*: it arises both spontaneously and in decorous order from the fullness of a generous heart.

That song, I know, cannot be sung at the Wakefield Hills Middle School. Not that or anything like it. Not in contemporary America, united solely by the conviction that no conviction must be permitted to unite us. But where there is nothing to celebrate and no one to worship, *something* must occupy our attention. The throne will not remain empty. Its most vulgar occupant is the itch. You *must* be at Times Square. Why? What does it mean? You *must* watch the television extravaganza. Why? What in that brew of folly, narcissism, mass marketing, and noise is worthy of honor or affection?

The Holy of Holies

The hunchback Quasimodo, hard of hearing from having rung the bells of Notre Dame de Paris all his life in the belfry, scrambles into the cathedral with the girl Esmeralda, whom he has spirited away from prison, where she was about to be executed for a murder she did not commit. He cries out, "Sanctuary, sanctuary!" He invokes the ancient right. Within the holy place, neither he nor Esmeralda can be taken captive. Up in that belfry towering high in the air, Esmeralda learns to see Quasimodo as her true friend.

"Put off thy shoes from off thy feet," says the Lord to Moses from the burning bush, "for the place whereon thou standest is holy ground." The holy is that mysterious and invaluable space set apart from politics, policemen, common drudgery, the passions of the mob, the humdrum habits of everyday life, chatter, buying and selling, making contracts and breaking them. When Quasimodo and Esmeralda are in the cathedral, we must not think that their safety depends upon an odd and hoary custom. The novelist Victor Hugo has penetrated to the essence of what the holy place is. The *right* of sanctuary, as a custom, flows from the *fact* of a sanctuary. The sanctuary is a place of freedom.

Why is this so?

Consider an ordinary middle-aged housewife, kneeling in prayer before bedtime. That is what C. S. Lewis gives us in *That Hideous Strength*. Mrs. Dimble, called "Mother Dimble" because, though she is childless, she has been like a mother to generations of her husband's students, has fallen to her knees, simply and matter-of-factly, while the sophisticated young Jane Studdock looks on in embarrassment. Jane has, as it were, fled to that place, Saint Anne's, as a sanctuary against the strange political machinations of the National Institute for Coordinated Experiments (the hideously named NICE). She does not yet know what prayer is all about. She is therefore both with Mrs. Dimble and not with her. She is a little bit like Esmeralda in the first fury of her salvation at the hands of Quasimodo.

It's clear that the truly free woman in that scene is not the agnostic Jane, wary, blushing, self-conscious, and feeling at once both superior and terribly inferior. It is Mrs. Dimble, who does not know that she is doing anything extraordinary. The silence of her prayer creates a holy space about her.

When you see someone kneeling, praying silently, you do not interrupt. You feel bound to respect the freedom of the praying person. You do not trudge over his silence with your muddy shoes. You do not ask about the stock exchange. You do not shoot a picture for the newspapers. You feel compelled to dismiss your compulsions. It is as if you had walked into a room in which two young lovers, holding hands, were whispering to each other. You are on holy ground.

Do not think that people race toward such freedom. The holy brings fear. It is a terrible thing to fall into the hands of the living

God, says the apostle to the Hebrews. Woe is me, cries the prophet, for now I must surely die, because I have looked upon the face of God. I am dust and ashes, says Job to the God who speaks to him from the whirlwind. Elijah hears the voice of God in a still small voice, like the whisper of the wind in dry leaves, and he hides his face. "Sell all that thou hast, and distribute unto the poor, and thou shalt have treasure in heaven," says Jesus to the young man tethered by his riches, "and come, follow me."

The sanctuary then is a place of both safety and danger; it is safe because it is holy and dangerous because it is free. It is the place where Quasimodo hangs by a bell rope two hundred feet above the square below. The men in Plato's cave, chained and all looking the same way at the shadows of transient things cast upon the wall, are emblems of the world and its compulsions. The holy is not found there. They think that they are beholding all that there is, but the real world is outside of that cave. The real world is a world of holiness, as broad and high as the heavens, and bathed in the brilliance of the sun. The false world of compulsions is the cubbyhole, cramped and dank. The sanctuary is to that world as the sun is to a glowworm, as a snow-capped mountain is to a speck of dust.

To enter the sanctuary, to fall upon your knees there, is to hobble or run to God, who is Love. And Love by its nature is not compelled. "Freely ye have received," says Jesus to the disciples he sends forth to preach, "freely give." And why not give? "For ye have not received the spirit of bondage again to fear," says Saint Paul, "but ye have received the Spirit of adoption, whereby we cry, Abba, Father."

All things pass away, but the word of God abides forever. The new Jerusalem, the city of God and the city of peace, the sanctuary of the blessed, flows with the water of life, freely. Its gates are never shut. The sounds of song and of feasting come from within. Outside, in that little pinhole animal pen called the world, the trains run on their tracks and the senators are voted in or out and the magazines cry out that you must do, must go, must buy, must sell, must read, must know, must worry; even as the beautiful people smile, they grind their teeth and their souls wail.

A king is giving a wedding feast for his son. He has sent his servants to call everyone to the wedding, but the people refuse. He fairly pleads with them to come, letting them know that the dinner is ready, the fatlings butchered and dressed. But they make light of it. They mock his servants. They beg off. One has a new business to run. One is flying to Atlanta. One is running for office. One has made an assignation with an escort service. One has papers to push. One has papers to pull. One has papers to shred. One has a wife to divorce. One has another man's wife to seduce. One can't hear the invitation over the noise of the television. One can't see the invitation behind the glare of the screen. One has forgotten even what it means to have a feast. They shut themselves out.

It is time, reader, to enter the sanctuary, to pray, to rejoice, to look upon the face of God, and to be free.

Epilogue

___

A Mystic with a Kite

We're on the flat top of a skyscraper, surmounted on its sides by parapets about three feet high. It's a breezy day, and a young man named Blue, who has in his life enjoyed both the freedom of riches and the freedom of owning nothing, has been painting a big box kite. Splashes of green are all over the deck and Blue's smiling face. Apparently Blue is going to fly that kite from the skyscraper. His more pragmatic friend describes the scene, as Blue imagines the *freedom* of matter itself:

> Blue announced his intention of flying the kite. That was one temptation he could never resist, he explained—the immediate flying of a new kite. "Who knows what a new kite will do? It may show powers undreamed of, special powers given it by accidental twists, fourth dimensional twists, with which it may pull the earth off its orbit, lug it into the way of the sun and planets, set them crossing, colliding, crashing, blasting the whole universe to pieces. That would be a kite! . . ." While he talked he fastened the kite by a slender strong cord that he unrolled from a great wooden spool. "What a kite! The least this green dragon can do is to pull me off the roof, pull me up over the city, up over the Great Lakes . . . up over Canada . . . up over Alaska . . . up over the North Pole!"

He was still chuckling, delighted with his fancies.

Meanwhile, he made the kite ready. He set it on top of his multicolored packing case. Then, giving himself plenty of free cord, he sprinted to the edge of the roof. I thought he would go over the parapet. But just as he reached the edge, the kite caught the wind and up it went in little spurts. The spool unwound madly as Blue fed the kite more freedom. He was still against the parapet. There came a lull in the kite's progress. Blue kept pulling in the cord and releasing it, pulling it in and releasing it, to force the kite upward. Suddenly, cramped for arm room, he jumped up to the top of the parapet. And there, leaning backward over the city, leaning with nothing holding him but the uncertain pull of the kite on a piece of string, with four hundred feet of frightful space beneath him, he began to sing!

Of course the author, Myles Connolly, is not recommending that we stand on the parapet of a skyscraper and fly kites, putting our lives in danger—or at least that not everybody should. What he's done is to craft a whimsical but complex and fruitful image of the freedom of a human soul, one that bears some careful analysis. Let's look at the items in the image, one by one.

First there is the sky. Nobody flies a kite indoors. Even if you could do it, why would you want to? The beauty of the kite is that it soars and flutters in the sky. It is man's fanciful creation of a bird, from sticks and paper and string. We can see Mr. Blue's bold green box dancing above with the wind, sometimes diving, sometimes climbing, always trembling, so frail and humble and yet so glorious. And yet there it is in the sky, that vast mysterious place of sun and wind, of clouds and rain, of light and darkness, of thunder and lightning. To be free is not to have *nothing* above you but to have *the skies* above you. To be imprisoned is to live out the curse of Charon, the ferryman of the wretched souls doomed in Dante's *Inferno* to the cramped funnel of Hell: *Non isperate mai veder lo cielo! Give up all hope to look upon the skies!* Or, since the Italian *cielo* means more than the stratosphere: *Give up all hope to look upon heaven.* That's appropriate, since Blue is a devout follower of Christ.

Then we have the string. "I've got no strings on me!" sings the foolish Pinocchio in the cartoon movie. That's quite in the spirit of Carlo Collodi's novel, which shows that Pinocchio is most the puppet and not a real boy when he goes his own way in heedlessness and folly. "I should be able to walk down Eaton Street wearing nothing but flip-flops and a smile," said the well-trained young feminist for my college's newspaper, heedless and self-absorbed and acknowledging no tie to God or her fellow man.

But Mr. Blue has a string. That string is, marvelous to consider, at once a cable and a lifeline and a wire of communication. The string is the means by which Blue partakes of the glorious voyage of the kite. He is in a way up in the sky with that kite. His spirit soars with it, because he, body and soul, is "tied" to the kite, and he submits to the initiative of the kite, as the kite submits to his giving it freer and freer play. There is no kite flying without that humble communicating string.

Then there is Blue himself and his posture. When he climbs on the parapet and leans backward over the city below, he is as dependent upon the kite as the kite is upon him. In fact, the two actions are one. It's the soaring pull of the kite that allows him to lean, and his leaning pull that allows it to soar all the higher. The image suggests the self-donation of love, of giving oneself away in greathearted freedom. We may well think here of devotion, in marriage or in worship. Mr. Blue is already thinking of those things, as we will learn.

Finally, there's the skyscraper. Blue might well have flown his kite in Central Park, but if he did that, we would be deprived of two important considerations.

The first is that freedom, like love, can never be safe. The hoarder cramps himself most of all. Scrooge in his countinghouse of a soul, says the grim ghost of Marley, is captive-bound and double-ironed. The scrambler after votes must lick the shoes of the people he courts. It isn't just that for love we should risk the world but also that without love we lose even what is good in the world. "Seek ye first the kingdom of God, and his righteousness," said Jesus, "and all these things shall be added unto you."

The second consideration is that freedom, again like love, is *for other people*. As Blue says to his skeptical friend who watches his kite flying, "Think of all the people uptown who are looking at it." Such a display of cheerful generous freedom should raise the eyes and the hearts of as many people as we can reach. Hence, the skyscraper finally serves a good end. It's not what goes on inside it that is important for Blue—the commercial labor. The skyscraper is good because it's got a great roof for kite flying for people to behold from down below. There is no such thing as love or worship that is merely private.

And that is why Blue's conversation, still up on that skyscraper, with his eyes trained on the kite, turns to marriage and family. "Can you tell me what happened to Saint Augustine's son?" he asks his friend, a stodgy publisher. The friend, revealing his ignorance and indifference, replies that he didn't know that Saint Augustine was married. "He wasn't married but he had a son," says Blue, who goes on to ask about the families of Saint Francis Borgia, Blessed Thomas More, and Saint Louis the King of France. "It's odd," he says, "that nowadays there's no special appeal to sainthood for the heads of families. The idea seems to be that, after a man is married, little else than an ordinary good Christian life is expected of him. In the ripe wisdom of noble husbandhood should lie, it seems to me, rare seeds of sanctity."

Think of *that* conversation, now, begun by that person, doing that mad and marvelous thing, in that place. What Blue is calling for is the soaring of love—and sanctity, without which the heights of love are unattainable—within the apparently humble and ordinary limits of marriage. And again we see that the string, the bond, the obedience, the fidelity, are not constrictions upon freedom but its very life. There is no kite without a string, and no love without a bond, and no holy freedom without the flinging away of oneself, in devotion to the God who sets us free.

Acknowledgments

I wish to thank here the people and the institutions without which this book would never have seen the light of day: my colleagues and friends at *Touchstone: A Journal of Mere Christianity*; the publishers at *Front Porch Republic*, where portions of these essays first appeared; those laymen and Dominicans at Providence College who have been examples for me of what a truly human education is; my mother and father, whose hard work and common sense and constant love made a genuine childhood possible for me, my brother, and my sisters; and my wife, Debra, who has done the same for our children. Special thanks are due to ISI Books, the finest American publisher of books for the common man, on education, politics, social life, economics, arts and letters, and religion, and to my editor, Jed Donahue, whose splendid recommendations and insights have been most effectual in transforming a series of arguments into a coherent whole.

Index

**INTERCOLLEGIATE
STUDIES INSTITUTE**
Educating for Liberty

ISI Books is the publishing imprint of the **Intercollegiate Studies Institute**, whose mission is to inspire college students to discover, embrace, and advance the principles and virtues that make America free and prosperous.

Founded in 1953, ISI teaches future leaders the core ideas behind the free market, the American Founding, and Western civilization that are rarely taught in the classroom.

ISI is a nonprofit, nonpartisan, tax-exempt educational organization. The Institute relies on the financial support of the general public—individuals, foundations, and corporations—and receives no funding or any other aid from any level of the government.